THE MOST SIGNIFICANT
PEOPLE,
PLACES, AND
EVENTS
IN THE BIBLE

THE MOST SIGNIFICANT
PEOPLE,
PLACES, AND
EVENTS
IN THE BIBLE

A QUICKVIEW GUIDE

CHRISTOPHER D. HUDSON

ZONDERVAN

The Most Significant People, Places, and Events in the Bible
Copyright © 2015 by Christopher D. Hudson

This title is also available as a Zondervan ebook.
Visit www.zondervan.com/ebooks.

Requests for information should be addressed to:
Zondervan, 3900 *Sparks Dr. SE, Grand Rapids, Michigan 49546*

Library of Congress Cataloging-in-Publication Data

Hudson, Christopher D.
    The most significant people, places, and events in the Bible : a quickview guide / Christopher D. Hudson.
       pages cm
    Includes index.
    ISBN 978-0-310-51835-8 (softcover)
    1. Bible—Outlines, syllabi, etc. 2. Names in the Bible. 3. Bible—History of Biblical events. I. Title.
  BS593.H84 2015
  220.9—dc23   2014024083

Cover design: Tammy Johnson
Cover photography or illustration: Christopher Hudson, www.HudsonBible.com
Interior illustration: Teresanne Russell
Interior design: Hudson & Associates, Inc.

Printed in China

19 20 21 /GPC/ 23 22 21 20 19 18 17 16 15 14 13 12 11 10 9 8 7 6 5 4 3

CONTENTS

To Caleb

ACKNOWLEDGMENTS

I am blessed to be surrounded by wonderful, Bible-loving people who share my passion for teaching God's Word and who made this book possible.

Special thanks go to Scott Rutherford: your research, concepts, ideas, and drafts were a gift and a blessing. Thank you, Janay Garrick, for helping me work through the writing and drafts. And I'm grateful for Nathan Barnes, whose valuable insights and review helped make this title better. Certainly, the greatest of thanks goes to Teresanne Russell, the talented artist who built each image in this book and in the *NIV QuickView Bible*.

Thank you to Madison Trammel and Nancy Erickson at Zondervan for believing in this book, as well as to the Zondervan Bible team (Chip, Melinda, Mike, Amy, Shari, Doris, and Jean), who supported and published the *NIV QuickView Bible*.

Last, thanks to my beautiful wife, Amber. You create the ultimate learning visual by displaying the love of Christ to me each day.

Bible Facts

NUMBER OF BOOKS IN THE BIBLE

66

NUMBER OF AUTHORS

40

39

Number of books in the Old Testament

Years to write
1,500

27

Number of books in the New Testament

Number of chapters in the Old Testament

1,189

NUMBER OF CHAPTERS IN THE BIBLE

Number of chapters in the New Testament

929

260

Number of verses in the Old Testament

Number of verses in the New Testament

31,173

NUMBER OF VERSES IN THE BIBLE

23,214

7,959

Number of questions in the Bible

3,294

Number of prophecies in the Bible

more than **8,000**

Number of commands in the Bible

6,468

Number of promises in the Bible

1,260

Psalm
119
LONGEST CHAPTER IN THE BIBLE

Psalm
117
SHORTEST CHAPTER IN THE BIBLE

Job
3:2
SHORTEST VERSE IN THE BIBLE

Joshua
8:33
LONGEST VERSE IN THE BIBLE

Many numbers are approximations.

LANGUAGES OF THE BIBLE = 3: HEBREW, ARAMAIC, GREEK

INTRODUCTION

The Bible is wonderfully complex. As the inspired Word of God, it is unlike any other book we might read, past or present. The Bible is an anthology of 66 books that were penned by at least 40 unique authors. While 39 books compose what Christians refer to as the Old Testament, the other 27 books compose the New Testament. Within both Testaments there is a wealth of complex and beautiful material to engage our hearts, minds, and spirits.

The Most Significant People, Places, and Events in the Bible: A QuickView Guide will help you make sense of the 31,000+ verses in Scripture. *The Quickview Guide* visually orients you to major characters, places, and events. Its infographics provide quick overviews alongside short articles that summarize key information. The book is divided into four helpful sections:

1. QuickView: Summary of the Bible. Whether you are new to the Bible or a regular reader, the images and articles in this section will give you a new perspective and handy overview of the Bible's 1,189 chapters.
2. QuickGlance: Bible Characters. This section provides fast facts and visual overviews of the real men and women in the Bible. By reading this section you'll be able to answer questions such as: Who were Abraham, Isaac, and Jacob? What similarities do Adam and Noah share? What does the Bible say about Jesus and the people who followed him?
3. QuickScan: Bible Places. Any good story is located in a specific place and time. QuickScan explores questions such as: What is the terrain of Israel? How about the climate in Egypt? Why didn't the Israelites get along with the people from Samaria? Getting to know the various settings and lands of the Bible will greatly enhance your understanding of each story.
4. QuickLook: Bible Events and Story Line. We have all heard the saying, "A picture speaks a thousand words." Learning experts report that 83 percent of human learning occurs visually, yet the Bible contains over 725,000 words. That's a lot of words! The QuickLook section provides pictures that "talk" and "teach," hopefully opening up new insights into the biblical story.

I hope you enjoy *The Most Significant People, Places, and Events in the Bible: A QuickView Guide* and its 100 new images that make God's message of hope in Scripture both engaging and accessible. Our Savior has come, and this is truly good news. Let's continue to read, engage, apply, and share the Bible.

Christopher D. Hudson

www.ReadEngageApply.com
Twitter: @ReadEngageApply
Facebook.com/Christopher.D.Hudson.books

CHAPTER 1

QUICKVIEW SUMMARY OF THE BIBLE

CREATION, FALL, PROMISE

The Bible is not written in the chronological style of many modern-day history books, so attempting to read it as such will be frustrating. The books of the Protestant Bible are arranged by subject, but if reassembled in chronological order, they disclose the progressive revelation of God, specifically the creation of humanity, our "fall" from a state of perfection, and the promise of God to send a Savior. The charts over the next few pages depict the key themes you'll find as the chronological story line of the Bible progresses.

Genesis and Job, the earliest story lines, reveal the power of God in his majesty and creation. Although sin enters the world through the first man and woman's disobedience and the lies of a serpent (Satan), God chooses a people to call his own and promises that salvation will one day come.

Shortly after Adam and Eve's first sin, God says to the serpent: "I will put enmity between you and the woman, and between your offspring and hers; he will crush your head, and you will strike his heel" (Genesis 3:15). This verse conveys the "curse," or the story of humanity's fall from a state of grace.

Genesis 3:15 also contains God's ultimate promise, that one of Adam and Eve's own offspring will "crush [the] head" of the serpent (Satan). Christians will later interpret this as a messianic prophecy, foretelling the coming of Jesus, the Messiah and Savior, who would reverse the catastrophic effects of the fall.

Where are we?

The further we get into the Bible, the more we learn about God and his plan for salvation. Here is where we are in the story.

Creation, Fall, Promise

A People Set Free

Bible Books Covered

Genesis

Job

Exodus

Leviticus

Numbers

Deuteronomy

(GENESIS, JOB)

Embracing
God's Promise

Kingdoms
in Tension

Exile and
Restoration

Promise
Fulfilled:
Jesus

New Life to
the World

What we learn about God and his plan

God is eternal and the Creator. Sin enters the world, but God begins to make his name great.

1–2 Samuel
1–2 Kings
1–2 Chronicles
Psalms
Proverbs
Ecclesiastes
Song of Songs
Isaiah
Jeremiah
Lamentations
Hosea
Amos
Jonah
Micah
Nahum
Habakkuk
Zephaniah

Ezra
Nehemiah
Esther
Ezekiel
Daniel
Joel
Obadiah
Haggai
Zechariah
Malachi

Matthew
Mark
Luke
John

Joshua
Judges
Ruth

Acts–Revelation

A PEOPLE SET FREE

The book of Genesis ends with Jacob—the heir of God's promises to Adam, Eve, and Abraham—and his sons resettling in Egypt. The first chapter of Exodus skips ahead 400 years, where we discover that the Hebrew people are now enslaved by the Egyptians. Exodus, Leviticus, Numbers, and Deuteronomy tell the story of God rescuing his people from slavery and their beginnings as a nation.

As is fitting with the Bible's overarching narrative, God is not only interested in giving his people physical freedom from their oppressors and a land of their own, but he is also interested in a relationship with them. Exodus 6:7 reveals his heart: "I will take you as my own people, and I will be your God." The Bible is the story of God's efforts to repair humanity's broken relationship with him, something that was damaged when Adam and Eve sinned in the garden.

These four books further introduce God's character. We discover his power through the plagues and miracles, learn of his jealousy revealed in his insistence that his people worship no other gods, and discover through the giving of the law what a relationship between God and humans looks like.

While viewing the Bible as a whole, we also see God making the concepts of sin and holiness more tangible. These themes will eventually reveal the need for a perfect sacrifice, the death of a Savior, to allow true freedom between God and his people.

Where are we?

The further we get into the Bible, the more we learn about God and his plan for salvation. Here is where we are in the story.

Creation, Fall and Promise

A People Set Free

Genesis
Job

Exodus
Leviticus
Numbers
Deuteronomy

Bible Books Covered

(EXODUS – DEUTERONOMY)

Embracing God's Promise

Kingdoms in Tension

Exile and Restoration

Promise Fulfilled: Jesus

New Life to the World

What we learn about God and his plan

God is holy and expects his people to be set apart from the world. Sin must be paid for by a blood sacrifice.

Embracing God's Promise	Kingdoms in Tension	Exile and Restoration	Promise Fulfilled: Jesus	New Life to the World
	1–2 Samuel			
	1–2 Kings			
	1–2 Chronicles			
	Psalms			
	Proverbs			
	Ecclesiastes			
	Song of Songs			
	Isaiah	Ezra		
	Jeremiah	Nehemiah		
	Lamentations	Esther		
	Hosea	Ezekiel		
	Amos	Daniel		
	Jonah	Joel		
	Micah	Obadiah	Matthew	
Joshua	Nahum	Haggai	Mark	
Judges	Habakkuk	Zechariah	Luke	
Ruth	Zephaniah	Malachi	John	Acts–Revelation

EMBRACING GOD'S PROMISE

At the conclusion of the book of Deuteronomy, the people of God wait at the threshold of the Promised Land. The books of Joshua, Judges, and Ruth record some of the early history of the people of Israel. After taking the land, they try to find their identity as God's "holy nation" (Exodus 19:6). From the opening battles of Jericho and Ai, the Israelites struggle to fully obey God, but they always find his blessing when they do. In Judges, a cycle begins to take shape as the people move in and out of obedience and sin.

While the Promised Land is a tangible gift, it is also symbolic of God's greater plan. God is moving his people toward a place where they can truly rest in his presence. In this overarching story of the Bible, God moves a people who wander as slaves in exile toward a place where they can encounter the fullness of joy at God's right hand (Psalm 16:11).

Through Joshua (the Hebrew name for Jesus), and ultimately through the reconciling work of Jesus Christ on the cross, people receive spiritual rest as they enter a restored relationship with God: "For if Joshua had given them rest, God would not have spoken later about another day. There remains, then, a Sabbath-rest for the people of God … Let us, therefore, make every effort to enter that rest, so that no one will perish by following their example of disobedience" (Hebrews 4:8–9, 11).

Where are we?

The further we get into the Bible, the more we learn about God and his plan for salvation. Here is where we are in the story.

Bible Books Covered

Creation, Fall and Promise

A People Set Free

Genesis
Job

Exodus
Leviticus
Numbers
Deuteronomy

Embracing God's Promise

Kingdoms in Tension

Exile and Restoration

Promise Fulfilled: Jesus

New Life to the World

What we learn about God and his plan

The people experience the consequences of sin. God delivers them so that they will serve him. The people repent and then fall back into sin.

1–2 Samuel
1–2 Kings
1–2 Chronicles
Psalms
Proverbs
Ecclesiastes
Song of Songs
Isaiah
Jeremiah
Lamentations
Hosea
Amos
Jonah
Micah
Nahum
Habakkuk
Zephaniah

Ezra
Nehemiah
Esther
Ezekiel
Daniel
Joel
Obadiah
Haggai
Zechariah
Malachi

Matthew
Mark
Luke
John

Acts–Revelation

Joshua
Judges
Ruth

KINGDOMS IN TENSION

For approximately 400 years, the Israelites live under tension created by a monarchy that the people choose over following God's plan. At times the tension is politically driven. Even when God's people live under one king in a unified kingdom, tensions arise between the different tribes and leaders. Israel's first king, Saul, attempts to kill his successor, David. Later, when David becomes king, his own son Absalom challenges his leadership. Even Solomon, who rules during a time of peace and great prosperity, encounters threats from his brother Adonijah and another key leader, Jeroboam. After Solomon's reign, the kingdom divides into the northern kingdom of Israel and the southern kingdom of Judah. These two nations wage war against each other, as well as against nations beyond their borders such as Assyria, Egypt, and Babylon.

Spiritual tensions exist when the nations vacillate between faithfully following God and rebelling against him. God allows wars and political turmoil to occur and raises prophets such as Hosea and Amos to call people to repentance. Hosea describes God's thoughts: "Will not Assyria rule over them because they refuse to repent?" (Hosea 11:5). During this time, God often uses conquering nations to drive the heart of his people back to him. Yet through it all, God remains long-suffering for his people, promising: "I will heal their waywardness and love them freely" (Hosea 14:4).

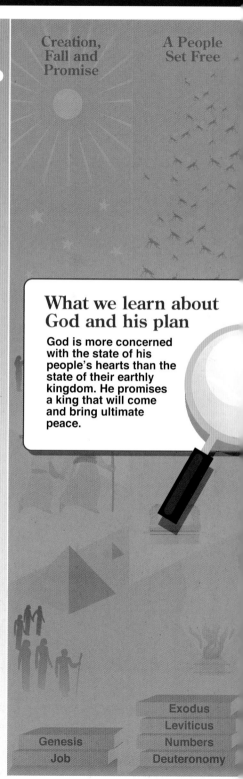

Where are we?

The further we get into the Bible, the more we learn about God and his plan for salvation. Here is where we are in the story.

© TheBiblePeople.com. Used by permission.

Creation, Fall and Promise

A People Set Free

What we learn about God and his plan

God is more concerned with the state of his people's hearts than the state of their earthly kingdom. He promises a king that will come and bring ultimate peace.

Bible Books Covered

Genesis
Job

Exodus
Leviticus
Numbers
Deuteronomy

EXILE AND RESTORATION

The books of Ezra, Nehemiah, and Esther trace the story of the Israelites living in exile, after the fall of both kingdoms. Biblical history from this time focuses on the people from the southern kingdom (Judah). The historical record of the northern kingdom of Israel is lost after it is conquered by the Assyrians in 722 BC.

Though the majority of God's people are in captivity, a small remnant remains in the ruins of Canaan. Under leaders like Ezra and Nehemiah, God slowly leads his people from exile back to the Promised Land to rebuild Jerusalem and the temple. He desires to restore his dwelling place among the Israelites.

In the books of Daniel, Joel, Obadiah, Haggai, Zechariah, and Malachi, God continuously raises up prophets to deliver his words of comfort and conviction to the Israelites in captivity and to those rebuilding the temple and city walls. God patiently urges his people to repent. He reminds them that he desires restoration with his creation despite their past disobedience. Though God is holy and just in his nature, he is also "gracious and compassionate, slow to anger and abounding in love" (Joel 2:13).

As the Israelites begin rebuilding the Promised Land, the prophets relate God's plan of ultimate restoration. They foretell the coming Messiah, or Savior, explaining that he will restore God's kingdom along with all of creation, reclaiming hearts for him.

Where are we?

The further we get into the Bible, the more we learn about God and his plan for salvation. Here is where we are in the story.

Creation, Fall and Promise

A People Set Free

What we learn about God and his plan

God will discipline his children for their sin but also graciously restore them. A fresh start is coming.

© TheBiblePeople.com. Used by permission.

Bible Books Covered

Exodus
Leviticus
Numbers
Deuteronomy

Genesis
Job

(HISTORY AND PROPHETS)

Embracing God's Promise

Kingdoms in Tension

Exile and Restoration

Promise Fulfilled: Jesus

New Life to the World

Embracing God's Promise	Kingdoms in Tension	Exile and Restoration	Promise Fulfilled: Jesus	New Life to the World
	1–2 Samuel			
	1–2 Kings			
	1–2 Chronicles			
	Psalms			
	Proverbs			
	Ecclesiastes			
	Song of Songs			
	Isaiah	Ezra		
	Jeremiah	Nehemiah		
	Lamentations	Esther		
	Hosea	Ezekiel		
	Amos	Daniel		
	Jonah	Joel		
	Micah	Obadiah		
Joshua	Nahum	Haggai	Matthew	
Judges	Habakkuk	Zechariah	Mark	
Ruth	Zephaniah	Malachi	Luke	
			John	Acts–Revelation

PROMISE FULFILLED: JESUS

Jesus, the Son of God, comes into the world thousands of years after God's first promise to send a Savior. When the first man and woman sin in the garden of Eden, they immediately destroy their connection to God, to one another, and to the created world around them. However, at the same moment that sin enters the world, the great promise of God enters the world, too.

Immediately after Adam and Eve sin, God says to Satan, our enemy (1 Peter 5:8): "I will put enmity between you and the woman, and between your offspring and hers; he will crush your head, and you will strike his heel" (Genesis 3:15). This verse contains both the "curse," or the story of humanity's fall from a state of grace, and God's great promise to send one who is greater than Satan. The Promised One who is greater than Satan is God's Son, Jesus. When God sends him into the world and he dies on the cross for our sins, he crushes the power of Satan to destroy our lives.

When the Son of God becomes a "son of man," born in a humble manger in the obscure town of Bethlehem, he begins the fulfillment of prophecies spanning hundreds of years before his birth. Ultimately, it is through Jesus' blood and his sacrificial death on the cross that "death has been swallowed up in victory" (1 Corinthians 15:54; Isaiah 25:8), providing for forgiveness of our sins and a way back to God.

Where are we?

The further we get into the Bible, the more we learn about God and his plan for salvation. Here is where we are in the story.

Creation, Fall and Promise

A People Set Free

What we learn about God and his plan

God offers a final and perfect solution for sin.

Bible Books Covered

Genesis
Job

Exodus
Leviticus
Numbers
Deuteronomy

Embracing
God's Promise

Kingdoms
in Tension

Exile and
Restoration

Promise
Fulfilled:
Jesus

New Life to
the World

1–2 Samuel
1–2 Kings
1–2 Chronicles
Psalms
Proverbs
Ecclesiastes
Song of Songs
Isaiah
Jeremiah
Lamentations
Hosea
Amos
Jonah
Micah
Nahum
Habakkuk
Zephaniah

Ezra
Nehemiah
Esther
Ezekiel
Daniel
Joel
Obadiah
Haggai
Zechariah
Malachi

Joshua
Judges
Ruth

Matthew
Mark
Luke
John

Acts–Revelation

NEW LIFE TO THE WORLD

The New Testament books of Acts – Revelation record the history of the early church, instructions on living as a citizen of the kingdom of God, and a vision of the new heavens and earth. The kingdom of God is a spiritual reality where God's presence dwells among his people. When asked about his kingdom, Jesus replies, "My kingdom is not of this world. If it were, my servants would fight to prevent my arrest by the Jewish leaders. But now my kingdom is from another place" (John 18:36). For now, the kingdom of God continues in the power and life of his people, the church, but the kingdom will not be fully realized until Jesus comes to earth a second time to usher in a new world.

The apostle Paul urges believers in Corinth to preach God's message of reconciliation — God's desire to restore humanity to right relationship with him, one another, and creation (2 Corinthians 5:17 – 21). Reconciliation is based on the good news that Jesus has conquered sin and death, removing the "wall of hostility" that sin had created between God and us. Jesus brings us near to God once again (Ephesians 2:13 – 14).

In Revelation, John describes the new world as a place where God's people will live without pain, suffering, or death. God "will wipe every tear from their eyes" (Revelation 21:4). Human beings will once again live in close relationship with our Creator in a world better than the one Adam and Eve knew in the garden of Eden.

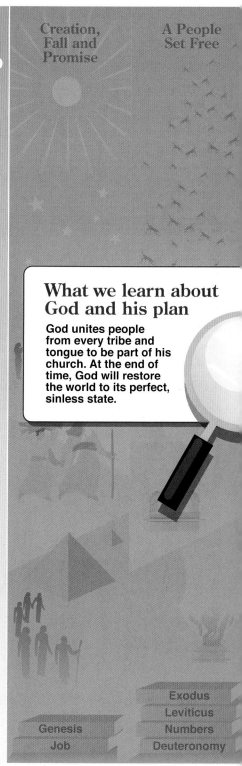

Where are we?

The further we get into the Bible, the more we learn about God and his plan for salvation. Here is where we are in the story.

Creation, Fall and Promise

A People Set Free

What we learn about God and his plan

God unites people from every tribe and tongue to be part of his church. At the end of time, God will restore the world to its perfect, sinless state.

Bible Books Covered

Genesis
Job

Exodus
Leviticus
Numbers
Deuteronomy

Embracing God's Promise

Kingdoms in Tension

Exile and Restoration

Promise Fulfilled: Jesus

New Life to the World

1–2 Samuel
1–2 Kings
1–2 Chronicles
Psalms
Proverbs
Ecclesiastes
Song of Songs
Isaiah
Jeremiah
Lamentations
Hosea
Amos
Jonah
Micah
Nahum
Habakkuk
Zephaniah

Ezra
Nehemiah
Esther
Ezekiel
Daniel
Joel
Obadiah
Haggai
Zechariah
Malachi

Matthew
Mark
Luke
John

Joshua
Judges
Ruth

Παῦλος

Acts–Revelation

WORDS OF THE BIBLE

Studying a list of the most frequently used words in different portions of Scripture highlights themes found within each of the Bible's sections. While story lines, settings, and people change as we read the Bible, one message remains constant: God lovingly reaches out to his people. The image below outlines the most frequently used words within each biblical section and will give you insights into each biblical section.

In the Pentateuch, we read about Moses leading the Israelites to the Promised Land. These books focus on sacrifices and holy festivals and remind God's people to depend on him.

In the Historical Books, the Israelites learn about life under an earthly king, while the temple is built as the central place of worship to their heavenly King.

The Wisdom Books outline the importance of being in right relationship with God. He seeks worshipers who long for righteousness with "a contrite heart" in place of empty sacrifices (Psalm 51:17).

The Major and Minor Prophets remind the Israelites of their covenant with God. God speaks to his people through prophets who recount the people's disobedience and disregard for his ways while faithfully urging them to return to him wholeheartedly.

The Gospels and the book of Acts introduce the life and saving work of Jesus, the Son of God. They focus on proclaiming God's kingdom come to earth and the mission of his church.

The Epistles, written to the early church, outline themes of grace and faith at work in God's people, who were commissioned

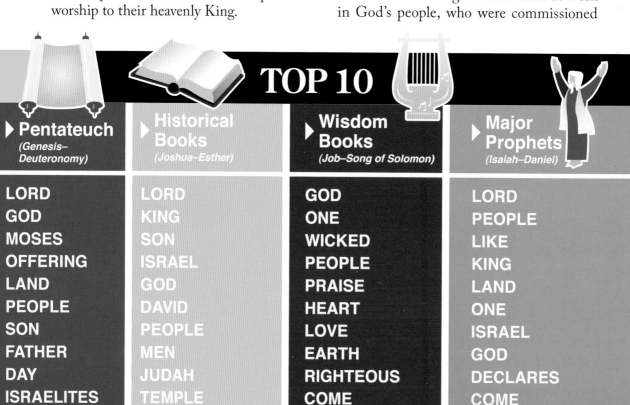

TOP 10

▶ Pentateuch (Genesis–Deuteronomy)	▶ Historical Books (Joshua–Esther)	▶ Wisdom Books (Job–Song of Solomon)	▶ Major Prophets (Isaiah–Daniel)
LORD	LORD	GOD	LORD
GOD	KING	ONE	PEOPLE
MOSES	SON	WICKED	LIKE
OFFERING	ISRAEL	PEOPLE	KING
LAND	GOD	PRAISE	LAND
PEOPLE	DAVID	HEART	ONE
SON	PEOPLE	LOVE	ISRAEL
FATHER	MEN	EARTH	GOD
DAY	JUDAH	RIGHTEOUS	DECLARES
ISRAELITES	TEMPLE	COME	COME

with proclaiming the gospel, or good news, of Jesus the Savior.

Finally, the book of Revelation contains prophecies about the end of the world as we know it, providing a vision of a new heaven and a new earth under God's good reign.

Frequency List

Each section of the Bible reveals different aspects of God, humanity, and the gospel message. These are the most commonly used words in different sections of the Bible. *

* Words such as pronouns, prepositions, articles and some other words have been intentionally omitted from the list.

The Bible as a whole:

TOP 20 WORDS

1. LORD
2. GOD
3. PEOPLE
4. ONE
5. KING
6. SON
7. ISRAEL
8. COME
9. LAND
10. DAY
11. JESUS
12. MAN
13. CAME
14. DAVID
15. MADE
16. HOUSE
17. GIVE
18. MOSES
19. JUDAH
20. SEE

TOP 10

▶ Minor Prophets (Hosea–Malachi)	▶ Gospels & Acts (Matthew–Acts)	▶ Epistles (Romans–Jude)	▶ Revelation
LORD	JESUS	GOD	GOD
PEOPLE	ONE	CHRIST	EARTH
DAY	GOD	LORD	ANGEL
GOD	MAN	ONE	SEVEN
ALMIGHTY	PEOPLE	JESUS	GREAT
ISRAEL	CAME	FAITH	SAW
LAND	SON	PEOPLE	COME
HOUSE	FATHER	SPIRIT	THRONE
NATIONS	LORD	KNOW	PEOPLE
DECLARES	DISCIPLES	LOVE	HEAVEN

CHAPTER 2

QUICKGLANCE BIBLE CHARACTERS

FIRST FATHERS: CREATION TO FLOOD

Shortly after being cast out of the garden, Adam and Eve lose their first two children. God condemns their son Cain to a life of wandering after he murders his brother, Abel, out of jealousy (Genesis 4:14–15). Then Adam and Eve have another son, Seth. It was during his life and the life of his son Enosh that people "began to call on the name of the LORD" (Genesis 4:25–26).

From the time of the creation of the world to the great worldwide flood, the Bible records ten generations. The Bible records very few details other than the names and ages of the next four generations after Seth, but there are some interesting glimpses provided about the lives of Enoch (seventh generation), Methuselah (eighth generation), Lamech (ninth generation),

Contrast of Characters

← .... Adam vs. Noah .... →

Genesis

Before he is created, the water covering the earth is gathered and reveals dry land *1:9–10*	**Before he leaves the ark, the floodwater covering the earth recedes and reveals dry land** *8:1–14*
Given the privilege of ruling over the animals as well as naming them *1:26; 2:19–20*	**Given the privilege of ruling over the animals as well as eating them** *9:2–3*
Told, along with Eve, to be fruitful and multiply *1:28*	**Told to be fruitful and multiply** *9:1,7*
Cares for the plants in the garden *2:15*	**Plants a vineyard after the flood** *9:20*
Eats the fruit and realizes he is naked *3:6–7*	**Drinks too much wine, becomes drunk and sleeps naked** *9:21*
His nakedness is covered by God *3:21*	**His nakedness is covered by two of his sons** *9:23*
His sin is passed on to his children *4:8*	**His sin is passed on to his son Ham** *9:22,24–25*
Has three sons: Cain, Abel and Seth *4:25*	**Has three sons: Shem, Ham and Japheth** *9:18*

and Noah and his sons (tenth and eleventh generations).

During that time, people live longer than they do today and have children at older ages. For example, the Bible records the child-bearing age to be between 65 and 187 years old. Enoch lives 365 years. The Bible says of him: "Enoch walked faithfully with God; then he was no more, because God took him away" (Genesis 5:24), suggesting that Enoch does not experience physical death.

Enoch's son Methuselah becomes the oldest person on record, living 969 years. Methuselah's son Lamech is the father of Noah, the man God chooses to save at the time of the great flood. When Noah is born, his father names him Noah, which sounds like the Hebrew word for "comfort," and says of him, "He will comfort us in the labor and painful toil of our hands caused by the ground the LORD has cursed" (Genesis 5:29).

By the time Noah becomes a man, the world is completely corrupt and God has decided to destroy it. God instructs Noah, a righteous man, to build an ark of cypress wood. God tells Noah to take himself, his family, and two of every type of animal onto the ark in order to save them from the catastrophic flood that God is sending (Genesis 6:14–20).

Age of Early Ancestors

The book of Genesis records the long lives of the early ancestors of faith; here are some of the better-known examples:

Ancestor	Bible Reference From Genesis	Age at Death
Adam	5:5	930
Seth	5:8	912
Methuselah	5:27	969
Noah	9:29	950

© Zondervan. Used by permission

ABRAHAM

Abraham is often referred to as the "father of the faith," while the New Testament points to Abraham as an example of being justified by faith, not works: "Abraham believed God, and it was credited to him as righteousness" (Romans 4:3; Genesis 15:6). Abraham's faith works itself out in his life. His faith is made evident in his deeds. James writes: Abraham's "faith and his actions were working together, and his faith was made complete by what he did" (James 2:22).

Abraham's journey requires great faith along the way. God first calls Abraham to leave his home country without telling him where he's supposed to go (Hebrews 11:8). God promises to bless him, to make his name great, and that the world will be blessed through his descendants (Genesis 12:1–3).

God then leads Abraham to the Promised Land. While there, Abraham builds an altar and calls on God. Abraham understands that following the living God is a relationship that involves both speaking and listening.

Abraham's journey isn't without its trials. At one point, Abraham is afraid that people will kill him for his beautiful wife, so he asks her to lie and say that she is his sister.

Throughout the years, God speaks to Abraham several times, confirming that he will bless him and his descendants. However, the promise doesn't become reality for many years. This wait tests Abraham's faith, especially since Abraham and his wife, Sarah, are getting old and they still do not have any children. How would they have descendants as numerous as the stars in the sky (Genesis 15:5) if they do not even have one child at this point in life?

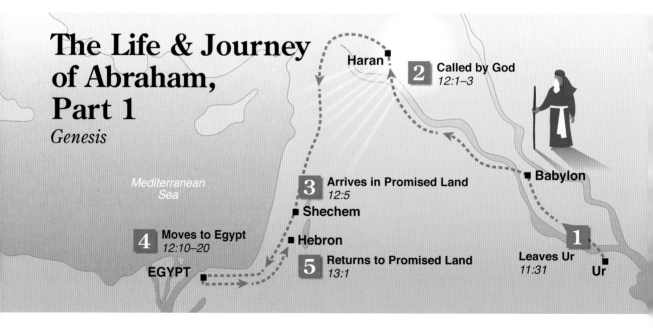

The Life & Journey of Abraham, Part 1
Genesis

Haran

2 Called by God
12:1–3

Babylon

Mediterranean Sea

3 Arrives in Promised Land
12:5
■ Shechem

4 Moves to Egypt
12:10–20

■ Hebron

5 Returns to Promised Land
13:1

EGYPT

Leaves Ur
11:31

1

Ur

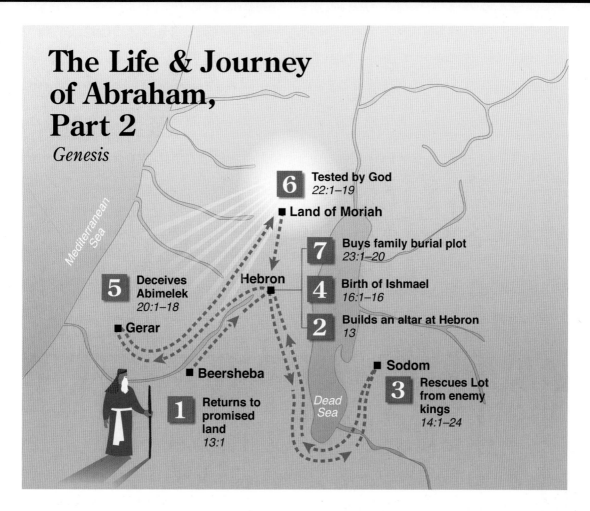

The Life & Journey of Abraham, Part 2

Genesis

6 Tested by God
22:1–19

■ **Land of Moriah**

7 Buys family burial plot
23:1–20

5 Deceives Abimelek
20:1–18

■ Gerar

Hebron

4 Birth of Ishmael
16:1–16

2 Builds an altar at Hebron
13

■ **Beersheba**

■ **Sodom**

3 Rescues Lot from enemy kings
14:1–24

Dead Sea

1 Returns to promised land
13:1

Mediterranean Sea

So Abraham's wife, Sarah, suggests that Abraham have children by her slave, Hagar. At the time, this is not an unusual cultural practice when a wife cannot conceive. Hagar gives birth to a son, Ishmael.

Twelve years later, God appears to Abraham and tells him Sarah will have a child. Sarah, who is 90 years old at the time, laughs at the idea. But one year later, she conceives and gives birth to Isaac, God's promised child.

God later puts Abraham's faith to the ultimate test when he asks him to sacrifice his "only son," Isaac (Genesis 22:2), foreshadowing the sacrifice God later makes with his one and only Son, Jesus (John 3:16). Abraham obeys God, but God stops him at the final moment.

ISAAC AND JACOB

When Abraham and Sarah are both elderly and without any children, God announces to Abraham that Sarah will give birth to a son and "that she will be the mother of nations" (Genesis 17:16).

When Isaac, the promised son, is still a young boy, God asks Abraham to offer his beloved son as a sacrifice. As Abraham is lifting his knife to sacrifice Isaac, an angel of the Lord prevents Isaac's death. A ram is provided to sacrifice in Isaac's place. Abraham names the place "The LORD Will Provide" (Genesis 22:1–14).

Once Isaac is a grown man, Abraham sends his servant back to his homeland to find a wife for Isaac. The servant returns with Rebekah, whom Isaac loves and marries (Genesis 24). Rebekah eventually gives birth to twins. Esau, meaning "hairy" or "rough," is the firstborn. Jacob, whose name means "grasps the heel" or "he deceives," is the younger twin. While Isaac favors Esau, Rebekah loves Jacob (Genesis 25:28).

Later, during a time of famine in the land, God appears to Isaac and repeats the same promise he made to Abraham years earlier: "I will bless you and will increase the number of your descendants for the sake of my servant Abraham" (Genesis 26:24).

Toward the end of his life, Isaac asks Esau to prepare a meal for him so he can bless him with his inheritance before he dies. Rebekah overhears this and plots with her favorite son, Jacob, to trick Isaac (Genesis 27:1–40). The deception succeeds, and Isaac blesses Jacob instead, leading to hostility between the twins.

Rebekah then sends Jacob away in order to avoid bloodshed (Genesis 27:41–28:5). While Jacob flees for his life, he dreams of a stairway to heaven. God reminds him again of the promise he first made to Jacob's grandfather, Abraham: "All peoples on earth will be blessed through you and your offspring. I am with you and will watch over you wherever you go, and I will bring you back to this land. I will not leave you until I

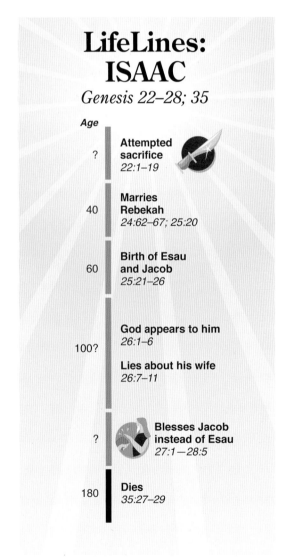

LifeLines: ISAAC

Genesis 22–28; 35

Age

?	**Attempted sacrifice** 22:1–19
40	**Marries Rebekah** 24:62–67; 25:20
60	**Birth of Esau and Jacob** 25:21–26
100?	**God appears to him** 26:1–6
	Lies about his wife 26:7–11
?	**Blesses Jacob instead of Esau** 27:1–28:5
180	**Dies** 35:27–29

have done what I have promised you" (Genesis 28:14–15).

When Jacob arrives in his mother's homeland, he meets Rachel and falls in love with her. Her father, Laban, tricks Jacob into marrying his other daughter, Leah. Jacob eventually marries both sisters, creating animosity between the two (Genesis 29:14–30). God blesses Leah with children while Rachel is childless. When Rachel finally conceives and has a son, Joseph, Jacob already has children with Leah and both servants.

After many years, Jacob's wealth and influence in the land grows, creating jealousy from his father-in-law's sons. God instructs Jacob: "Go back to the land of your fathers and to your relatives, and I will be with you" (Genesis 31:3). En route to his homeland, Jacob has an unusual encounter with God, who apparently appears to Jacob as a man. The two wrestle and Jacob refuses to let go until God blesses him. God indeed blesses him, changing his name to Israel, for he has "struggled with God" (Genesis 32:22–32; 35:9–15).

When Jacob nears his homeland, he hears a report that Esau is coming to meet him with a small army. Jacob sends peace offerings ahead to his brother, and the two reconcile (Genesis 33).

Jacob eventually has 12 sons and a daughter. His firstborn son with Rachel, Joseph, ultimately saves the entire family during a time of famine. At the end of his life, Jacob resettles his family in Egypt. Before he dies, he insists that his descendants return his remains to Canaan (Genesis 46–49).

LifeLines: JACOB
Genesis 25–49

Age

Trades for Esau's birthright
25:29–34

Steals Esau's blessing
27:1–41

Flees from Esau
28:1–5

Dreams of a stairway to heaven
28:10–22

Marries Leah
29:16–27

Marries Rachel
29:28–30

Sons are born
29:31—30:24

Flees from Laban
31

Wrestles with God
32:22–27

Name changed to Israel
32:28–32; 35:9–15

Reunites with Esau
33

Devastated by the loss of Joseph
37:31–35

Sends sons to Egypt during famine
42:1–5

Reunites with Joseph
46:29–30

130   **Resettles in Egypt**
47

147   **Dies**
47:28; 49:29–33

WIVES OF THE PATRIARCHS

Sarah, Rebekah, Leah, and Rachel are the women who marry the patriarchs—Abraham, Isaac, and Jacob—the "founding fathers" of the faith. Their unique stories illustrate how women play an important role in the unfolding of God's plan of salvation.

Sarai is elderly and childless when God changes her name to Sarah, the "mother of nations," and gives her the promise of a son (Genesis 17:15–21). Sarah demonstrates great faith and joy in God's promises and blessing. At the age of 90, she gives birth to Isaac, the "child of promise" (Genesis 18:1–15; 21:1–7; Galatians 4:28).

Abraham sends his servant in search of a wife for Isaac (Genesis 24). God faithfully leads him to Rebekah, the woman God has chosen as a wife for Isaac and mother to Jacob, who becomes the father of the twelve tribes of Israel.

Leah and Rachel are sisters who marry the same man—Jacob. Their relationship overflows with both jealousy and blessing. Laban, their father, tricks Jacob into marrying his older daughter, Leah, before he can marry the woman that he loves, Laban's younger daughter, Rachel (Genesis 29). Leah gives birth to six sons, including Judah (Genesis 29:31–35; 30:9–12, 16–20), whose lineage includes Jesus Christ. Rachel bears two sons (Genesis 30:22–24; 35:18), including Joseph, who later rises to power in Egypt, saving his brother Judah and the rest of his family during a severe famine (Genesis 37–50).

Wives of the Patriarchs
Genesis

Abraham Marries **SARAH**	Isaac Marries **REBEKAH**	Jacob Marries **LEAH & RACHEL**	
God changes her name from Sarai to Sarah and calls her the "mother of nations" *17:15–16*	Marries Isaac, son of Abraham *24:67*	Leah's father tricks Jacob into marrying her before he can marry the woman he loves, Rachel, her younger sister *29: 23–30*	Becomes the second wife of Jacob, son of Isaac; is loved more than Leah, Jacob's first wife *29:30*
Gives birth to Isaac in her old age *17:17; 21:1–3*	Gives birth to twin boys, Esau and Jacob *25:24–26*	Gives birth to six sons *30:19–20*	Gives birth to first son, Joseph *30:22–24*
Lives to be 127 years old *23:1–2*	Assists Jacob in stealing Esau's firstborn birthright *27:6–10*	Gives birth to one daughter *30:21*	Dies while giving birth to second son, Benjamin *35:16–18*

JOSEPH

Joseph's life illustrates how trusting God through dark times can lead to greater blessing.

From a young age, Joseph learned from God that he was destined for great things. Joseph dreamed that his brothers and father would one day bow to him (Genesis 37:1–11). However, Joseph needed to continue to trust God through some difficult trials before realizing those visions.

When Joseph was young, his brothers sold him into slavery to rid themselves of his annoying habits (Genesis 37:12–28). Soon after Joseph received a promotion in his slave master's house, he became the victim of more adversity. His master's wife falsely accused Joseph of trying to seduce her, and Joseph was thrown into prison. But the Lord was with him (Genesis 39).

In prison, Joseph earned a position of notice. He helped his fellow prisoner, Pharaoh's cupbearer, by interpreting his dreams. But when the cupbearer was released from prison, he neglected to mention Joseph to Pharaoh. Joseph remained a prisoner for two more years (Genesis 40; 41:1).

Ultimately, Joseph was given the opportunity to successfully interpret Pharaoh's dreams. Pharaoh then promoted him as second-in-command over all Egypt (Genesis 41), providing a great example of how "in all things God works for the good of those who love him, who have been called according to his purpose" (Romans 8:28).

In the end, Joseph's family did bow to him. When it happened, Joseph demonstrated incredible humility and faith by assuring them that what they had planned for evil — his brothers selling him into slavery — God had meant for good.

Hebrews 11:22 tells us, "By faith Joseph, when his end was near, spoke about the exodus of the Israelites from Egypt and gave instructions concerning the burial of his bones." To the end of his life, Joseph continued to trust God and believe God's promise that the Israelites would one day return to the Promised Land.

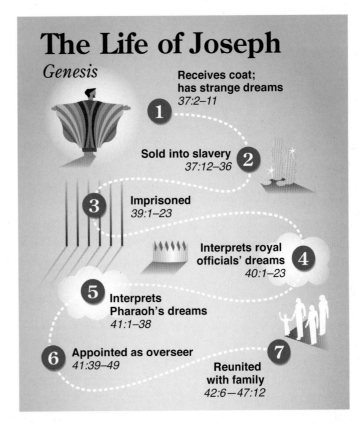

The Life of Joseph
Genesis

1 Receives coat; has strange dreams
37:2–11

2 Sold into slavery
37:12–36

3 Imprisoned
39:1–23

4 Interprets royal officials' dreams
40:1–23

5 Interprets Pharaoh's dreams
41:1–38

6 Appointed as overseer
41:39–49

7 Reunited with family
42:6—47:12

MOSES

The life of Moses demonstrates God's ability to deliver his people. Moses' story begins when Pharaoh, the Egyptian king, feared that the growing number of Hebrew slaves would become a threat to national security. As a result, he ordered that all newborn Hebrew baby boys be thrown into the Nile (Exodus 1:15–16, 22). Moses' parents "hid him for three months after he was born, because they saw he was no ordinary child, and they were not afraid of the king's edict" (Hebrews 11:23). But when it became too difficult to hide the baby, Moses' mother sent him floating safely down the river in a basket. Eventually, in an ultimate irony, Pharaoh's daughter found Moses and adopted him (Exodus 2:5–10).

Later, Moses fled Egypt after killing an Egyptian who mistreated an Israelite slave (Exodus 2:11–15). Moses "refused to be known as the son of Pharaoh's daughter. He chose to be mistreated along with the people of God rather than to enjoy the fleeting pleasures of sin" (Hebrews 11:24c–25). He fled to Midian, where he married, had children, and worked for forty years tending flocks

(Exodus 2:16–22), a job considered detestable by the Egyptians. Without photographs or modern-day manhunts that could locate him, Moses seemed content to put Egypt and his crime behind him while living in exile.

When God called Moses to return to Egypt and lead the Israelites out of slavery, Moses resisted and even doubted his own qualifications (Exodus 3–4). But God proved that he can use even unqualified people like Moses to accomplish great things. Moses had to rely completely on God's power to deliver the Israelites. God would tell the apostle Paul many years later, "My power is made perfect in [your] weakness" (2 Corinthians 12:9).

From the time of Moses' call, his life became a cycle of trusting God's word, delivering God's messages, and witnessing God doing what he said he would do. Obeying God often placed Moses in difficult situations, but God always delivered him. God presented the Law—his legal and moral expectations—through Moses and used him to guide the Israelites through the wilderness before they entered the Promised Land (Exodus 20).

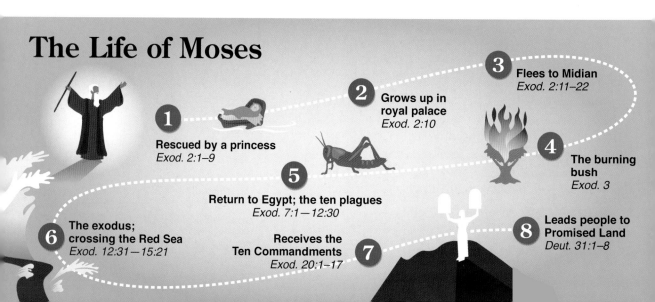

The Life of Moses

1 Rescued by a princess
Exod. 2:1–9

2 Grows up in royal palace
Exod. 2:10

3 Flees to Midian
Exod. 2:11–22

4 The burning bush
Exod. 3

5 Return to Egypt; the ten plagues
Exod. 7:1–12:30

6 The exodus; crossing the Red Sea
Exod. 12:31–15:21

7 Receives the Ten Commandments
Exod. 20:1–17

8 Leads people to Promised Land
Deut. 31:1–8

JOSHUA

Joshua, the son of Nun from the tribe of Ephraim, is a helper of Moses, the leader of Israel (Numbers 11:28). When God commands Moses to send 12 spies to explore the Promised Land, Moses chooses Joshua to represent the tribe of Ephraim (Numbers 13:8, 16).

Upon their return, all of the spies agree that the land is indeed full of promise. Ten of the spies are afraid that the peoples living in the land are too powerful to overcome. These spies discourage the Israelites from entering the Promised Land, while Joshua and Caleb encourage the people to obey God (Numbers 14:5 – 9).

Out of fear, the Israelites follow the advice of the cowardly spies. Because of their lack of faith, they spend 40 years wandering in the wilderness. Of the 12 spies, only Joshua and Caleb live to enter the Promised Land (Numbers 14:10 – 38).

Before his death, Moses names Joshua his successor, the new leader of Israel (Numbers 27:12 – 23). Shortly after Moses dies, God promises to be with Joshua and give him victory (Joshua 1:1 – 9). In response, the Israelites promise to follow and obey Joshua just as they did Moses (Joshua 1:16 – 18).

Joshua then leads the Israelites through a series of military victories to conquer the Promised Land. God repeatedly shows his miraculous power and grace by knocking down the enemy's walls and causing the sun to stand still at Joshua's request (Joshua 6; 10:7 – 14). However, Joshua also suffers defeat when the Israelites disobey God by keeping treasure they were told to destroy (Joshua 7).

Out of his love for God, Joshua leads the Israelites to renew their covenant with God (Joshua 8:30 – 35). Once they conquer the Promised Land, Joshua assembles the Israelites, encouraging them to fear and serve God only (Joshua 24).

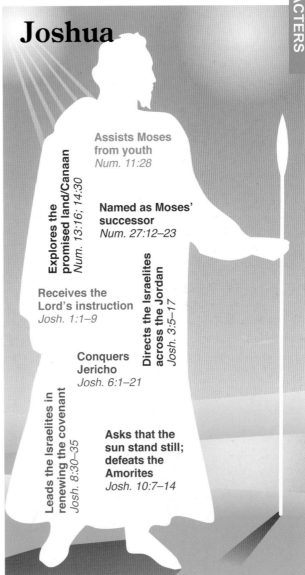

Joshua

Assists Moses from youth
Num. 11:28

Explores the promised land/Canaan
Num. 13:16; 14:30

Named as Moses' successor
Num. 27:12–23

Receives the Lord's instruction
Josh. 1:1–9

Directs the Israelites across the Jordan
Josh. 3:5–17

Conquers Jericho
Josh. 6:1–21

Leads the Israelites in renewing the covenant
Josh. 8:30–35

Asks that the sun stand still; defeats the Amorites
Josh. 10:7–14

TWO PROPHETESSES

Miriam and Deborah are among the most significant women in the Old Testament. Miriam plays an important role during Israel's exodus from Egypt, while Deborah leads Israel during a period when judges oversee the people.

Miriam is born toward the end of Israel's 400 years of slavery in Egypt (Numbers 26:59). Being the sister of both Moses and Aaron, Miriam functions as a leader (Micah 6:4) and prophetess in her own right (Exodus 15:20–21). During the exodus, after God miraculously parts the Red Sea so the Israelites can escape their Egyptian pursuers (Exodus 14), Miriam and Moses compose a song. They lead the Israelite community in praising God for his unfailing love: "I will sing to the LORD, for he is highly exalted. Both horse and driver he has hurled into the sea" (Exodus 15:1).

Like the lives of all of Israel's leaders, Miriam's life has its share of success and failures. For example, when Miriam and Aaron jealously challenge Moses' leadership, God strikes her with leprosy. After Moses intercedes for her, God then heals her (Numbers 12:1–15). Later, during the recounting of the law, Moses warns the Israelites, "Remember what the LORD your God did to Miriam" (Deuteronomy 24:9).

Deborah leads the people of Israel during a time when they are suffering under Canaanite oppression due to their sin (Judges 4:1–4). Under God's direction, she orders Barak to lead an army against Israel's enemies. When Barak refuses to go into battle without her, she bravely agrees to go with him. In battle, she prophesies that the honor for defeating the Canaanites will go to a woman, a key prophecy that is later fulfilled (Judges 4:17–22).

Like Miriam and Moses after the parting of the Red Sea, Deborah and Barak compose a song of victory. Once again, God's leaders guide the Israelites in worshiping and thanking him for saving them from their enemies.

Two Prophetesses

MIRIAM	DEBORAH
Prophet and singer *Exod. 15:20–21*	**Judge in Israel** *Judg. 4:4–5*
From the Levite tribe; sister of Moses and Aaron *Num. 26:59*	**Prophet** *Judg. 4:14*
Leader during the exodus from Egypt *Micah 6:4*	**Poet and singer** *Judg. 5*

RUTH AND BOAZ

During the time of the judges in Israel, a Moabite woman named Ruth marries an Israelite man who had immigrated to Moab.

When her husband dies, Ruth selflessly chooses to return to Judah with her widowed mother-in-law, Naomi, rather than remarry in her home country. Ruth promises Naomi: "Your people will be my people and your God my God" (Ruth 1:16).

When the women arrive in Bethlehem, Ruth provides for Naomi and herself by gleaning in barley fields. (God's law required harvesters to leave the edges of their fields and the gleanings of the harvest for the poor and foreigners within their borders. See Leviticus 19:9-10.)

Ruth gleans from a field owned by Boaz, who notices Ruth and inquires about her. When he hears about Ruth's kindness to Naomi, he feeds her and invites her to gather with his workers and takes steps to ensure her safety (Ruth 2:1–17).

As the story unfolds, it is discovered that Boaz is a guardian-redeemer for Naomi's family (Ruth 2:20). A guardian-redeemer is a close relative who can buy the land owned by a deceased relative and take on the responsibility and privilege of marrying, caring for, and having children with the widow of that relative. In a bold move prompted by Naomi, Ruth approaches Boaz for help (Ruth 3:1–15).

After ensuring that no closer relatives desire to redeem her, Boaz marries Ruth (Ruth 4:1–12). They have a son, Obed, who becomes the grandfather of King David. As a result, Ruth, the Moabite, takes her place in the lineage of Jesus Christ (Matthew 1:5).

The Story of Ruth and Boaz
Ruth

Ruth, a young widow, devotes her life to her mother-in-law, Naomi
1:16–18

Ruth leaves her country of Moab and moves to Bethlehem with Naomi
1:22

Boaz notices Ruth and gives her protection in his fields
2:8–9

Ruth gleans from the fields of Boaz to feed herself and Naomi
2:17–18

Boaz becomes guardian-redeemer of Naomi's estate and marries Ruth
4:9–12

Ruth gives birth to Obed, grandfather of David
4:13–17

SAMUEL

Samuel is both a prophet and the last of Israel's judges. God uses Samuel to institute the monarchy and anoint Israel's first two kings, Saul and David.

With the powerful ministry Samuel experiences, the miraculous circumstances surrounding his birth are not surprising. His mother, Hannah, longs for a child but is unable to conceive. One day, when her husband goes to worship in the temple, Hannah prays so fervently that the temple priest, Eli, believes she is intoxicated. In her prayer, she promises to dedicate her child to the Lord if he blesses her with a son (1 Samuel 1:1 – 18). A year later, Hannah gives birth to Samuel, a name that sounds in Hebrew like "heard by God" (1 Samuel 1:19 – 20). True to her promise, Hannah raises Samuel until he is weaned, then presents him to Eli to be raised in the Lord's house.

Samuel grows up in a time when it is rare to hear the word of the Lord or experience visions (1 Samuel 3:1). While he is still a young boy, God speaks audibly to Samuel, calling him by name while he sleeps. Eli instructs him to respond, "Speak, LORD, for your servant is listening" (1 Samuel 3:9). The Lord tells Samuel that he is going to bring judgment on Eli's house because Eli's sons are wicked and Eli has not rebuked them. Even though Samuel is afraid to tell Eli the message, he faithfully recounts all that God has said (1 Samuel 3:11 – 18).

By the time Samuel reaches adulthood, he is recognized as a prophet throughout Israel (1 Samuel 3:19 – 21). During the early years of his ministry, the Philistines, Israel's longtime enemies, defeat Israel and capture the ark of the covenant. The ark represents the presence of God among the Israelites. Eli and his two sons die the day the ark is captured (1 Samuel 4). When the Philistines place the ark inside their temple, God breaks a statue of their god and strikes the Philistines with tumors (1 Samuel 5:1 – 6). After seven months, the Philistines return the ark to the Israelites (1 Samuel 6). At this time, Samuel instructs the people to stop worshiping other gods and return to the Lord (1 Samuel 7:2 – 6). Then the Philistines attack again. This time, as Samuel prays and offers a sacrifice, the Israelites rout the Philistines (1 Samuel 7:7 – 14).

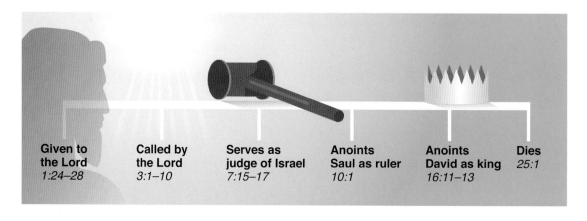

Given to the Lord	Called by the Lord	Serves as judge of Israel	Anoints Saul as ruler	Anoints David as king	Dies
1:24–28	*3:1–10*	*7:15–17*	*10:1*	*16:11–13*	*25:1*

Samuel's service as Israel's last judge includes traveling a circuit from his home to cities throughout Israel, judging the disputes of the people. He also builds an altar to the Lord in his hometown of Ramah (1 Samuel 7:15–17). When Samuel ages, he appoints his sons to lead Israel, but they don't follow his ways (1 Samuel 8:1–3). Because of this, the Israelites ask Samuel to appoint a king (1 Samuel 8:4–5). Samuel is reluctant to do so, but the Lord tells him, "Listen to them and give them a king" (1 Samuel 8:22). God also tells Samuel to warn the people of the consequences for having a human rule over them as king (1 Samuel 8:6–18).

God instructs Samuel to anoint a young Benjamite named Saul as leader over Israel. After anointing Saul as Israel's first king, Samuel directs Saul toward a group of prophets. God gives Saul another heart, and he begins to prophesy (1 Samuel 10:5–9). At first, Saul is reluctant to accept his appointment. He tries to hide when Samuel announces his kingship to the people, but God reveals where he is hiding (1 Samuel 10:17–24). The people receive Saul as king. Samuel explains to them "the rights and duties of kingship" and then records the words on a scroll and deposits the scroll before the Lord (1 Samuel 10:25).

After Saul squelches an Ammonite attack on an Israelite city, Samuel announces his retirement from his service to Israel. In his farewell speech, Samuel gives the Israelites a chance to lodge any complaints they may have against him concerning his service as Israel's leader. They confirm that they have none. Samuel is blameless. He reminds the Israelites that they have done evil in asking for a king. He closes his speech with these words: "Be sure to fear the LORD and serve him faithfully with all your heart; consider what great things he has done for you. Yet if you persist in doing evil, both you and your king will perish" (1 Samuel 12:24–25).

As Samuel steps back, Saul assumes full authority and responsibility over Israel. Although Saul begins his kingship in humility, a turning point comes when he disobeys the Lord during a battle against the Philistines. Saul doesn't wait for Samuel's arrival and offers sacrifices, something only priests are allowed to do (1 Samuel 13:1–12). When Samuel arrives, he rebukes Saul and tells him that the Lord will replace him with a king who will follow after God's "own heart" (1 Samuel 13:13–14).

When God rejects Saul as king, Samuel mourns for him (1 Samuel 15:35–16:1). God soon instructs Samuel to anoint David as king (1 Samuel 16). Although Samuel anoints David while he is still a young man, David does not become king for several years. Rather, David serves under Saul until Saul becomes so jealous of him that David is forced to flee. When David flees from Saul, he goes to Samuel and his prophets in Ramah (1 Samuel 19:18). Saul and his men find out where David is, but when they arrive in Ramah to kill him, they are overwhelmed by the Spirit of God and prophesy along with Samuel (1 Samuel 19:19–24). The lives of both David and Samuel are spared. In the end, Samuel dies several years before the Israelites install David as their new king (1 Samuel 25:1).

SAUL

The Israelites demand a king to rule over them (1 Samuel 8). Though displeased that they've sought an earthly king, God instructs Samuel to anoint one to rule his people. At the age of 30, Saul becomes king (1 Samuel 13:1). While his reign began with optimism, his life spiraled into disaster.

While out looking for his father's lost donkeys, Saul crosses paths with Samuel, who anoints Saul as king (1 Samuel 9:1–10:1). When Samuel assembles the Israelites to introduce their new leader to them, Saul shows timidity by hiding among the community's baggage (1 Samuel 10:20–24). Although the majority of the Israelites embrace Saul, a few "troublemakers" refuse to accept him as king (1 Samuel 10:24–27a). Saul demonstrates restraint before his opposition (1 Samuel 10:27b).

The early part of Saul's reign is marked by success as he leads Israel in a series of military victories over the surrounding pagan nations (1 Samuel 14:47–48). However, during a battle against the Philistines, Saul reveals his growing arrogance. Rather than following God's instructions and patiently waiting for Samuel, Saul breaks God's command by offering a sacrifice before the battle (1 Samuel 13:1–15).

Saul and his son Jonathan lead Israel into further military victory, but Saul continues to ignore the Lord's instructions. The Lord tells Samuel, "I regret that I have made Saul king, because he has turned away from me and has not carried out my instructions" (1 Samuel 15:11). Samuel tells Saul that the Lord has rejected him as Israel's king.

When the Spirit of the Lord departs from Saul, an evil spirit torments him (1 Samuel 16:14). David, the young man Samuel anoints to replace Saul, is summoned to play the harp to soothe the distraught king (1 Samuel 16:19–23). At first, Saul is delighted with David. However, as David grows in prominence, Saul grows increasingly jealous. Without the Spirit of the Lord and Samuel's counsel, Saul becomes desperate. He eventually drives David away and attempts to kill him (1 Samuel 19:8–17), orders priests murdered (1 Samuel 22:6–19), and consults a medium (1 Samuel 28:3–25). In the end, Saul is defeated in battle and commits suicide (1 Samuel 31:1–6).

King Saul
1 Samuel

- Anointed by Samuel as king 10:1,21–24
- Filled with the Spirit of God 10:10–13
- Disobediently offers burnt offering 13:1–15
- Tormented by an evil spirit 16:14–23
- Tries to kill David 19:8–24
- Orders murder of priests and people of Nob 22:14–19
- Consults a medium 28:3–25
- Commits suicide 31:4–6

DAVID

David, the second king of Israel, is one of the most central figures in the Old Testament. As a musician, he had many psalms attributed to him, but perhaps most significant is the fact that God makes a covenant with him. God promises him: "Your house and your kingdom will endure forever before me; your throne will be established forever" (2 Samuel 7:16). This kingdom is ultimately established by Jesus, the Savior, who would come through David's bloodline one thousand years later.

Born into humble circumstances, David is the youngest son of Jesse, a lowly shepherd from Bethlehem in the tribe of Judah (1 Samuel 17:12–15). While David is still a young man, God sends the prophet Samuel to anoint him as the next king of Israel (1 Samuel 16:1–13).

Before he replaces Saul as king, David serves in Saul's court as a skilled harpist (1 Samuel 16:14–23). Later, David rises to military fame when he boldly steps forward to face Goliath, a nine-foot-tall giant. David says, "You come against me with sword and spear and javelin, but I come against you in the name of the LORD Almighty" (1 Samuel 17:45a). With the Lord's help, David defeats Goliath with just a shepherd's sling (1 Samuel 17:48–49).

David initially finds great approval from King Saul, who sends him on a number of military campaigns. However, jealousy begins to grip Saul when Israelite women sing a song that portrays David as a greater war hero than Saul (1 Samuel 18:5–9). As Saul's jealousy grows, he attempts to kill David several times. Jonathan, Saul's son, eventually warns David to flee for his life.

While hiding in the wilderness, David attracts an army of followers. On at least two occasions, David has the opportunity to kill Saul while the king pursues him (1 Samuel 24:1–12; 26:2–25). He refuses to do so because Saul is "the LORD's anointed" (1 Samuel 26:11). Saul's jealousy becomes his own undoing and ultimately destroys him.

When David is 30 years old, he becomes king of all of Israel (2 Samuel 5:1–5). He then embarks on a number of successful military campaigns, including the capture of Jerusalem, which becomes his capital city (2 Samuel 5:6–10).

While David's reign includes many great successes, it also has its share of failures. David's first attempt to transport the ark of the covenant meets with the Lord's disapproval because he doesn't follow the Lord's instructions (2 Samuel 6:1–11; see Exodus 25:10–15). At one point, one of David's sons, Absalom, leads a rebellion against him (2 Samuel 15). David's most well-known failure is his adulterous affair with Bathsheba. When he learns that she is pregnant, David arranges for her husband Uriah's death in order to cover it up (2 Samuel 11:1–21). David then marries Bathsheba, through whom Solomon is later born.

Not long before the end of his reign, David becomes prideful and angers God by conducting a census of his fighting men (2 Samuel 24). As a result of David's sin, God sends a plague that kills 70,000 Israelites. God does not withdraw the plague until David repents and offers a sacrifice.

David, like all human leaders, often fails in his struggle against sin. After each failure, David experiences true repentance and wholeheartedly returns to God. After committing adultery with Bathsheba, he writes Psalm 51, a psalm of human repentance and God's unfailing grace. David understands that God will not turn away from "a broken and contrite heart" (Psalm 51:17) but will instead cleanse him from all unrighteousness. Despite David's failures, he is described as a man "after [God's] own heart" (1 Samuel 13:14; Acts 13:22).

Toward the end of his life, David desires to build a permanent temple for the Lord, but the Lord tells him that his son Solomon will do so (1 Chronicles 22:7–10). David establishes Solomon as his heir and gives him instructions regarding the building of the temple. David dies at age 70 after ruling Israel for 40 years.

Hundreds of years later, Matthew records the genealogy of Jesus, noting David, Bathsheba ("Uriah's wife"), and their son Solomon in the Messiah's bloodline (Matthew 1:6). Throughout Jesus' ministry he is called the "son of David," which refers to the covenant the Lord made with David, and indeed the Savior, the "Root of Jesse" (Isaiah 11:1; Romans 15:12), would come through David's offspring. Jesus is the perfect son of righteousness who will succeed where David failed in establishing God's righteous kingdom.

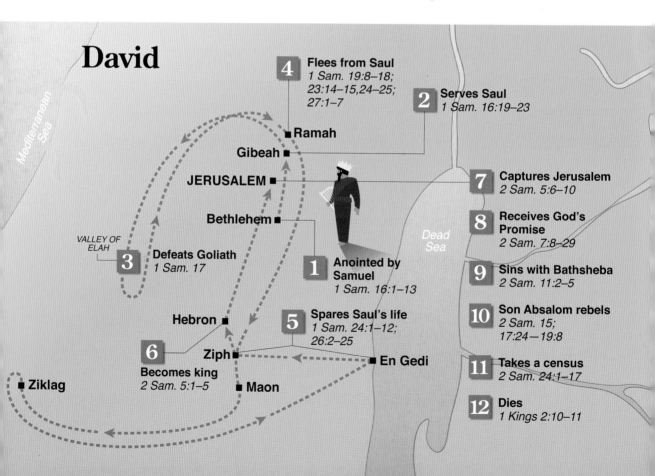

David

4 Flees from Saul
1 Sam. 19:8–18; 23:14–15, 24–25; 27:1–7

2 Serves Saul
1 Sam. 16:19–23

Mediterranean Sea

■ Ramah

Gibeah ■

JERUSALEM ■

7 Captures Jerusalem
2 Sam. 5:6–10

Bethlehem ■

8 Receives God's Promise
2 Sam. 7:8–29

VALLEY OF ELAH

3 Defeats Goliath
1 Sam. 17

1 Anointed by Samuel
1 Sam. 16:1–13

Dead Sea

9 Sins with Bathsheba
2 Sam. 11:2–5

Hebron ■

5 Spares Saul's life
1 Sam. 24:1–12; 26:2–25

10 Son Absalom rebels
2 Sam. 15; 17:24–19:8

6 Becomes king
2 Sam. 5:1–5

Ziph ■

■ En Gedi

11 Takes a census
2 Sam. 24:1–17

■ Ziklag

■ Maon

12 Dies
1 Kings 2:10–11

SOLOMON

Solomon is the son of King David and Bathsheba. David names him as his successor, and he becomes Israel's third king. The biblical books of Song of Songs, Ecclesiastes, and most of Proverbs are attributed to him.

Although David had promised Bathsheba that her son would become Israel's next king (1 Kings 1:17), his ascension to the throne was not without challenge.

One of David's other sons (Adonijah) attempts to claim the throne before David publicly announces his choice of successor. Several of David's key advisors, including the military leader Joab and the priest Abiathar, support Adonijah's claim to the throne. The prophet Nathan and the priest Zadok are among Solomon's supporters. Nathan encourages Bathsheba to pose the question of succession directly to King David, who responds by having Solomon crowned king (1 Kings 1:28–40).

Solomon is initially merciful to Adonijah but later has him executed when Adonijah persuades Bathsheba to request that Solomon allow him to marry one of David's concubines—a request Solomon equates with an effort to claim the throne. Solomon also executes Joab according to his father David's wishes, but he allows Abiathar to live because he carried the ark of the covenant during David's reign (1 Kings 2:13–34).

During the early years of Sol-

omon's reign, he lives a life of obedience to God as illustrated by the thousand burnt offerings he offers God at Gibeon. That night, the Lord appears to him in a dream and tells him, "Ask for whatever you want me to give you." God is pleased when Solomon asks for wisdom to rule God's people and promises to also give him great wealth, honor, and—if he will walk in obedience—long life (1 Kings 3:3–15).

Solomon illustrates his God-given wisdom when he is asked to rule between two women who both claim the same baby as their own. Solomon offers the solution of

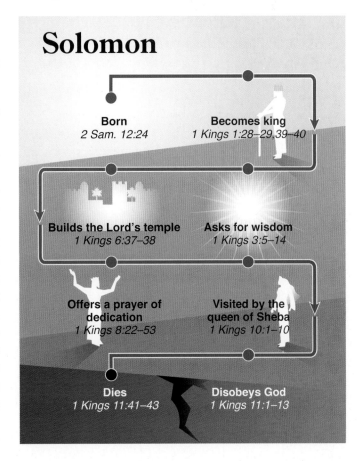

Solomon

Born
2 Sam. 12:24

Becomes king
1 Kings 1:28–29,39–40

Builds the Lord's temple
1 Kings 6:37–38

Asks for wisdom
1 Kings 3:5–14

Offers a prayer of dedication
1 Kings 8:22–53

Visited by the queen of Sheba
1 Kings 10:1–10

Dies
1 Kings 11:41–43

Disobeys God
1 Kings 11:1–13

cutting the baby in half and giving half to each of them. When one woman agrees to the suggestion and the other is willing to give up the baby in order to spare the child's life, Solomon discerns the true mother's heart and orders that the baby be given to her (1 Kings 3:16–28).

Solomon acquires great learning about a wide variety of subjects, including zoology and botany. He also writes songs and speaks 3,000 proverbs, many of which were recorded in the Bible. First Kings 4:31 describes Solomon as "wiser than anyone else." People, including great rulers like the Queen of Sheba, come to hear Solomon's wisdom (1 Kings 4:29–34; 10:1–10).

One of Solomon's greatest accomplishments is the construction of the temple. It takes seven years to build and requires thousands of laborers, including many whom Solomon conscripts into service. While Solomon is having the temple built, the word of the Lord comes to him and reaffirms the promise to Solomon's father, David. God promises to be with the Israelites and not to abandon them (1 Kings 6:11–13).

After Solomon completes the temple and its furnishings, he has the ark of the covenant brought into the temple. When the ark is placed in the Holy of Holies, the Lord fills the temple with his glory in the form of a cloud so thick that the priests are unable to conduct their normal duties (1 Kings 8:6–12). Solomon then prays and dedicates the temple, calling on the Lord to hear his people's prayers when they call on him from the temple (1 Kings 8:22–61).

Bylines

The number of psalms attributed to each writer*

David	73
Asaph	12
The sons of Korah	11
Solomon	2
Moses, Heman, Ethan	1 each

*49/Unknown

© Zondervan. Used by permission

While the early part of Solomon's reign was marked by obedience to God, the latter part of his reign is marked by disobedience. Solomon marries hundreds of foreign women — something Israelites are forbidden to do — and allows them to continue worshiping their foreign gods. Solomon eventually allows his heart to be led astray and follows foreign gods such as Ashtoreth, Chemosh, and Molech (1 Kings 11:1–8).

Because of Solomon's unfaithfulness, God informs him that his son will rule over a divided kingdom. Ten of Israel's twelve tribes will be ruled by one of Solomon's subordinates, leaving Judah to be ruled by Solomon's descendants (1 Kings 11:9–13, 26–40). This word is fulfilled during the reign of Solomon's son Rehoboam.

ENEMIES OF ISRAEL

From the period of slavery in Egypt to the time when exiled Judahites are allowed to return to Jerusalem and rebuild the temple, Israel is almost always under threat from her enemies.

After the exodus, Israel experiences times of war and periods of alliance with Egypt (1 Kings 3:1).

When the Israelites enter Canaan, or the Promised Land, a number of Canaanite nations naturally oppose them. Israel completely destroys some of these nations while struggling with others throughout much of their history. God's people continue to have periodic warfare against the Canaanites, Midianites, Philistines, and Ammonites.

During the time of the divided kingdom, the Assyrians become a most feared enemy. They conquer the northern kingdom of Israel (2 Kings 15:29; 17:1–6). The Babylonians then conquer the southern kingdom of Judah (2 Kings 24–25). Eventually the Medes and the Persians conquer the Babylonians (Daniel 5:30–31).

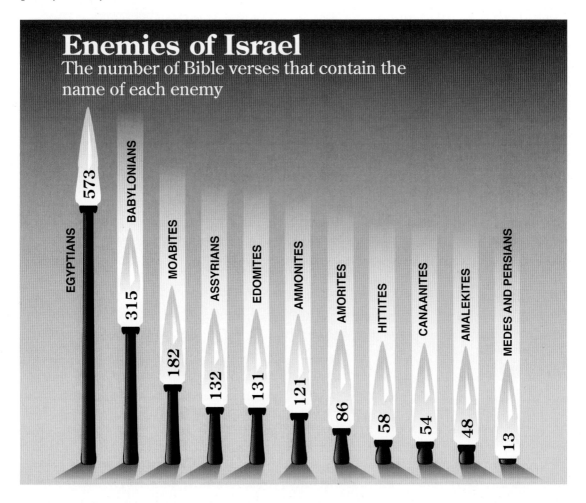

Enemies of Israel
The number of Bible verses that contain the name of each enemy

- EGYPTIANS — 573
- BABYLONIANS — 315
- MOABITES — 182
- ASSYRIANS — 132
- EDOMITES — 131
- AMMONITES — 121
- AMORITES — 86
- HITTITES — 58
- CANAANITES — 54
- AMALEKITES — 48
- MEDES AND PERSIANS — 13

ELIJAH

BIBLE CHARACTERS

Elijah is most famous for his ascension into heaven in a whirlwind (2 Kings 2:1–11). In the New Testament, Jesus refers to Elijah when he is rejected by the people in his hometown (Luke 4:25–26). Jesus also speaks with Elijah and Moses during his transfiguration (Matthew 17:1–13).

Elijah serves as Israel's prophet during the reign of King Ahab, the most evil of Israel's kings. Ahab worships Canaanite gods and marries Jezebel, a Phoenician princess who attempts to kill all of God's prophets, including Elijah (1 Kings 16:29–33; 18:4). Throughout his ministry, Elijah continues to confront Ahab.

In one situation, Elijah informs Ahab that there will be no rain in Israel until God chooses to send it. After Elijah delivers this difficult message, the word of the Lord directs him to hide in the Kerith Ravine, where ravens are sent to feed him (1 Kings 17:1–6). God then directs Elijah to the home of a widow, who has barely enough food for herself and her son. Nevertheless, the widow shows great faith by sharing her limited resources with Elijah. He prophesies that her food supply will miraculously last until the rain returns (1 Kings 17:8–16). After some time passes, the widow's son dies. Elijah prays, and God restores the boy's life (1 Kings 17:17–24).

After three years, Elijah confronts Ahab again and challenges 450 of his pagan prophets to a spiritual battle on Mount Carmel (1 Kings 18:16–40). Elijah challenges them to call on the name of their god, Baal, asking him to consume a prepared sacrifice by fire. The pagan prophets call out for hours, but Baal does not respond. When Elijah prays, God immediately sends fire from heaven that consumes the sacrifice. Elijah orders the execution of all the prophets of Baal. After this, the rain returns to Israel (1 Kings 18:45).

Jezebel renews her threat to kill Elijah, and he flees to Mount Horeb, where he experiences the presence of God (1 Kings 19:7–18).

Elijah

Taken to heaven
2 Kings 2:1–11

Announces a
great drought
1 Kings 17:1

Witnesses
God's presence
1 Kings 19:9–16

Fed by ravens
1 Kings 17:2–6

Flees from Jezebel
1 Kings 19:1–5

Helps a widow at
Zarephath
1 Kings 17:8–24

Defeats prophets of
Baal and Asherah
1 Kings 18:16–40

ISAIAH

Isaiah is recorded as one of Israel's most significant prophets. This is due not only to the length of his ministry (he prophesied during the reigns of at least four kings—Uzziah, Jotham, Ahaz, and Hezekiah) but also to the lengthy book that bears his name. The book of Isaiah contains some of the Bible's best-known prophecies about the coming Messiah (Isaiah 53).

Early in his ministry, Isaiah sees an incredible vision. He declares, "I am ruined!" because he has seen the Lord and he is "a man of unclean lips" (Isaiah 6:1–5). In the vision, one of the seraphim (six-winged creatures) cleanses him of his sin by placing a live coal on his lips (Isaiah 6:6–7). After this, Isaiah demonstrates faithfulness by agreeing to proclaim God's message to the Israelites, even though God shows him that most of the people will not receive the message until after they have suffered the consequences of their rebellion (Isaiah 6:8–13).

A theme throughout his early ministry is God's judgment. Isaiah warns the Israelites against depending on foreign alliances for protection instead of relying on God. During Isaiah's lifetime, the neighboring kingdom of Assyria rises to power and presents a constant threat to Israel. The prophet warns the Israelites of the consequences of rebelling against God and encourages them to remain obedient to God and to let him cleanse them (Isaiah 1).

Isaiah's later ministry is largely devoted to Messianic prophecy, future events, and proclaiming hope for God's people. Many of Isaiah's prophecies have been fulfilled, such as his prophecies that the Babylonians (a minor power during the time of Isaiah's ministry) would rise as an empire, take the people of Israel into exile (Isaiah 39:3–8), and later fall into obscurity (Isaiah 14:22–23). Isaiah also foretells God's continued protection of Israel and the destruction of Assyria, the major power in the region at the time (Isaiah 37:21–38). Although the Bible does not record the death of Isaiah, Jewish tradition indicates he may have been sawn in two because of his faithful prophecies.

Isaiah
Isaiah

Sees a vision concerning Judah and Jerusalem *1:1–9*

Responds to God's call *6:1–8*

Prophesies against Babylon *13*

Foretells the fall of King Sennacherib of Assyria *37:5–7*

Prophesies about Jesus *53:5–9*

Anointed with the Spirit of the Lord *61:1–3*

JEREMIAH

Jeremiah, known as the "weeping prophet," has a broken heart over the unrepentant hearts of his people and the eventual fall of his beloved homeland, Judah. The prophet cries out, "My eyes fail from weeping, I am in torment within; my heart is poured out on the ground because my people are destroyed" (Lamentations 2:11a).

When God calls a teenage Jeremiah to become a prophet, he objects: "I do not know how to speak; I am too young" (Jeremiah 1:6). But God promises to give Jeremiah the words he is to say (Jeremiah 1:7–9). God also warns Jeremiah that he will face great opposition for most of his life. He promises, however, to be with Jeremiah and to rescue him (Jeremiah 1:17–19).

Jeremiah's early prophecies proclaim God's judgment on the people of Israel and Judah for forsaking God and worshiping the gods of Canaan and the surrounding nations. Jeremiah declares that God will punish the hypocrites who allow themselves to be physically circumcised but lack tender hearts (Jeremiah 9:25–26).

As God had forewarned, Jeremiah and his prophetic message are not well received. Judah's priests and prophets call for his death. He is beaten (Jeremiah 20:1–2). He is forbidden from entering the temple and must send messages through his assistant, Baruch (Jeremiah 36:4–7). King Jehoiakim burns the scrolls containing Jeremiah's prophecies (Jeremiah 36:20–32). Jeremiah is imprisoned (Jeremiah 37:11–16; 38:6–13).

Some people speculate that Jeremiah writes the book of Lamentations during Jerusalem's fall to the Babylonian Empire in 586 BC. The book is filled with the heartbreak of a prophet watching his beloved homeland fall beneath the power of a pagan empire. Yet even in this book of despair, there is a message of hope: "Because of the LORD's great love we are not consumed, for his compassions never fail. They are new every morning" (Lamentations 3:22–23a).

When Jerusalem is conquered and destroyed by the Babylonians (as prophesied), Jeremiah is forcibly taken to Egypt by fleeing Judahites. He warns them that Egypt will also be conquered by Babylon and spends his remaining years fulfilling God's calling for him to be a prophet to "the nations" (Jeremiah 46:1), prophesying against Egypt, Babylon, and other nations.

While exiled in Babylon, the prophet Daniel finds renewed hope in the words of Jeremiah's prophecy: The people will return to their homeland after seventy years in captivity (Jeremiah 25:11–14; Daniel 9:2).

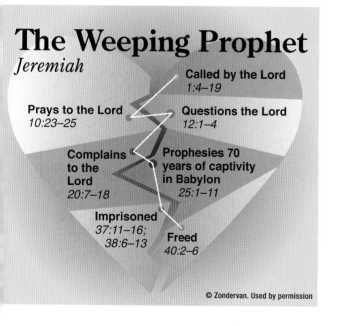

The Weeping Prophet
Jeremiah

Called by the Lord
1:4–19

Prays to the Lord
10:23–25

Questions the Lord
12:1–4

Complains to the Lord
20:7–18

Prophesies 70 years of captivity in Babylon
25:1–11

Imprisoned
37:11–16;
38:6–13

Freed
40:2–6

© Zondervan. Used by permission

DANIEL

Daniel's life spans the entire period of Judah's captivity in Babylon. He serves as God's messenger to God's people as well as to their ruling nations. Although he often brings a message of God's judgment, he is well received by Babylon's kings because of his integrity and ability to interpret dreams and visions.

Daniel, born into Israelite nobility, is still a young man when he is taken into captivity in Babylon. For three years, he and a select group of Israelite young men receive training in the Babylonian language and customs. This training prepares them to serve within the Babylonian government.

Following his years of training, Daniel occupies the role of one of Babylon's "wise men" (Daniel 2:13, 17–18). On one occasion, the Babylonian king threatens to execute his wise men if they fail to accurately describe to him a certain perplexing dream he's had. God saves Daniel and his companions by revealing both the details and the meaning of the king's dream to Daniel (Daniel 2). After this, Daniel rises to a position of greater prominence.

Daniel and his companions' faithfulness to the God of Israel is continually tested. The government leaders create laws that violate God's first commandment: "Have no other gods before me" (Exodus 20:3). At one point, Daniel's companions are thrown into a furnace; on another occasion, Daniel is thrown into a lions' den. In each instance, they remain faithful to God, and God rescues them (Daniel 3; 6).

In his later years, Daniel receives a series of fantastic visions about the future (Daniel 9–12). Jesus refers to Daniel's prophecies when he teaches his disciples about the end times (Matthew 24:15; see Daniel 9:25–27; 11:31).

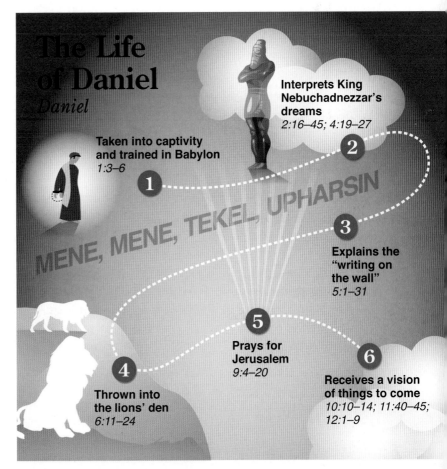

The Life of Daniel
Daniel

MENE, MENE, TEKEL, UPHARSIN

1 Taken into captivity and trained in Babylon
1:3–6

2 Interprets King Nebuchadnezzar's dreams
2:16–45; 4:19–27

3 Explains the "writing on the wall"
5:1–31

4 Thrown into the lions' den
6:11–24

5 Prays for Jerusalem
9:4–20

6 Receives a vision of things to come
10:10–14; 11:40–45; 12:1–9

JESUS

Jesus is the central figure of the Bible and is known as the Christ, the Anointed One, the Savior, and the Messiah. In keeping with traditional Christian teaching of the trinity, Jesus *is* God and was *with* God at the creation (John 1:1). He remains with God now as the world awaits his second coming (Hebrews 1:3).

The Old Testament records numerous prophecies that point toward Jesus' future coming as a fully divine human being in order to deliver God's people from sin and death.

Jesus, God's only Son, is born to a virgin named Mary in a Bethlehem stable (Luke 2:1–7). The Bible records that only a few people, such as Mary and possibly her husband Joseph, understood Jesus' identity as "the Son of the Most High" who would be given "the throne of his father David" (Luke 1:29–33). For the most part, Jesus grows up hidden from the public eye. However, even when he is a child, his wisdom astonishes religious leaders (Luke 2:41–52).

Around the age of 30, Jesus begins his public ministry. He is baptized by his cousin John the Baptist in the Jordan River. The Holy Spirit descends on him like a dove as a voice from heaven says, "This is my Son ... with him I am well pleased" (Matthew 3:13–17). Jesus then goes into the desert for forty days, where he resists Satan's temptations. After this time, Jesus visits the local synagogue, unrolls the scroll of Isaiah, and announces his mission to usher in "the year of the Lord's favor" through proclaiming good news to the poor and freedom for the oppressed (Luke 4:18–19). The onlookers are shocked when Jesus says, "Today this scripture is fulfilled" (Luke 4:21).

For approximately three years, Jesus teaches God's Word (often using parables), performs miracles, and ministers compassionately to people. He feeds thousands with five loaves of bread and two fish, heals the sick, gives sight to the blind, and causes the lame to walk and the mute to speak. He walks on water (Mark 6:45–53) and raises people from the dead (Luke 7:11–16; John 11:11–44).

He confronts religious leaders who manipulate people for profit (Mark 11:15–19) and keep rules rather than show compassion (Mark 3:1–6). Jesus foretells his own suffering, death, and resurrection (Mark 8:31–33; 9:30–32; 10:32–34) as he offers himself as the atoning sacrifice for the world's sins (Hebrews 10:12).

Jesus is eventually arrested, convicted for blasphemy by Jewish courts, sentenced to death by the Roman authority, and crucified between two thieves. He suffers and dies on the cross and is placed in a tomb carved out of a rock. After three days, he rises from the dead. More than 500 people see Jesus after his resurrection.

Before he ascends to heaven, Jesus reaffirms his authority and promise to send the Holy Spirit to empower his followers to continue his mission by preaching "the gospel to all creation" (Mark 16:15) and "baptizing them in the name of the Father and of the Son and of the Holy Spirit" (Matthew 28:19).

Life and Ministry of Jesus Christ

MAJOR LIFE EVENTS

Born
Luke 2:1–7

Visits temple as a boy
Luke 2:41–52

Enters Jerusalem for Passover
John 12:12–18

Shares the Last Supper with his disciples
Mark 14:22–26

SPIRITUAL BATTLE

Tempted by the devil
Matt. 4:1–11

Cures demon-possessed man
Mark 5:1–20

THE APOSTLES

Calls the first disciples
Matt. 4:18–22

Appoints 12 apostles
Mark 3:13–19

Predicts Peter's denials
Luke 22:31–34

WATER IN THE LIFE OF CHRIST

Changes water into wine
John 2:1–10

Walks on water
Mark 6:45–53

Baptized by John
Matt. 3:13–17

Washes the disciples' feet
John 13:3–10

MIRACLES

Feeds more than five thousand people
Matt. 14:13–21

Transfigures
Matt. 17:1–8

Throws money changers from the temple
Mark 11:15–19

Heals a faithful woman
Mark 5:25–34

Curses a fig tree
Mark 11:12–14,20–25

Brings a widow's son back to life
Luke 7:11–17

Brings Lazarus back to life
John 11:11–44

TEACHING OF JESUS

Models how to pray
Matt. 6:5–15

Teaches on the power of prayer
Luke 11:5–13

Teaches on discipleship
Mark 8:34–38

Blesses children
Mark 10:13–16

Foretells his death and resurrection
Mark 8:31–33; 9:30–32; 10:32–34

Promises to send the Holy Spirit
John 14:1–21

POWERFUL PEOPLE INTERACTIONS

Meets Zacchaeus
Luke 19:1–10

Saves an adulterous woman
John 8:1–11

DEATH AND RESURRECTION

Arrested
Matt. 26:47–56

Dies by crucifixion
John 19:16–37

Raises from death to life
Matt. 28:1–10

Appears to the apostles after his resurrection
Luke 24:36–49

Ascends to heaven
Mark 16:19

PETER (SIMON)

Simon Peter is a fisherman on the Sea of Galilee when he meets Jesus. Peter's brother, Andrew, first hears John the Baptist declare Jesus as "God's Chosen One" (John 1:34). Andrew immediately runs to find Peter and tells him they have found the Messiah. Jesus then meets them on the shore and calls Peter to leave behind his fishing nets and follow him to "fish for people" (John 1:35–42; Luke 5:1–11).

During his ministry, Jesus often travels with only Peter, James, and John. Because of this, Peter experiences many miracles. For example, Peter is present when Jesus raises a synagogue leader's daughter from the dead (Luke 8:51–56). Peter is one of the few to witness Jesus speaking with Moses and Elijah. During this experience, Peter also hears God affirm that Jesus is his Son (Mark 9:2–7).

In many instances, Peter acts as a courageous disciple. When the disciples see Jesus walking on the water and mistake him for a ghost, Peter has the boldness to come when Christ calls him. He begins to walk on the water, too (Matthew 14:22–31). When Jesus asks his disciples who they believe he is, Peter is the first to answer. He proclaims that Jesus is "the Messiah, the Son of the Living God" (Matthew 16:16). It is here that Jesus gives Simon the name Cephas (in Hebrew) or Peter (in Greek), meaning "rock" (Matthew 16:18).

While Peter is a key leader in Jesus' inner circle, he also has his struggles. For example, Peter debates with Jesus about whether the Messiah must suffer and die (Matthew 16:21–23). In addition, though Peter says he will never forsake Jesus, he denies Jesus three times after Jesus is arrested (Mark 14:27–31, 69–72).

After Jesus dies and rises from the dead, he speaks with Peter. Though Peter feels great shame for denying Jesus, Jesus forgives him and reaffirms Peter's calling to tend and feed God's flock (John 21:15–19) before ascending to heaven.

Later, Peter is with the other disciples on the day of Pentecost as the Holy Spirit is released. That day, Peter preaches a message that leads 3,000 people to follow Christ (Acts 2). Peter's ministry is marked

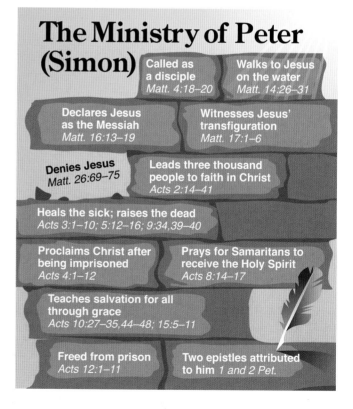

The Ministry of Peter (Simon)

Called as a disciple
Matt. 4:18–20

Walks to Jesus on the water
Matt. 14:26–31

Declares Jesus as the Messiah
Matt. 16:13–19

Witnesses Jesus' transfiguration
Matt. 17:1–6

Denies Jesus
Matt. 26:69–75

Leads three thousand people to faith in Christ
Acts 2:14–41

Heals the sick; raises the dead
Acts 3:1–10; 5:12–16; 9:34,39–40

Proclaims Christ after being imprisoned
Acts 4:1–12

Prays for Samaritans to receive the Holy Spirit
Acts 8:14–17

Teaches salvation for all through grace
Acts 10:27–35,44–48; 15:5–11

Freed from prison
Acts 12:1–11

Two epistles attributed to him 1 and 2 Pet.

by miracles, including healings (Acts 3:1–10; 5:12–16; 9:32–35) and raising a girl from the dead (Acts 9:36–41). Peter is arrested twice for preaching about Jesus (Acts 4:1–4; 12:3–5) and is freed from his second imprisonment by an angel (Acts 12:3–19).

As an early church leader, Peter is among the first to preach Christ beyond the Israelite community (Acts 10). He also defends the teaching that non-Jewish Christians do not need circumcision—the outward sign of following Jewish religious laws—in order to be saved (Acts 15:6–11).

The early Christians preserve two short epistles written by Peter. The first epistle (1 Peter), written to Jewish Christians, includes teachings on the church's response to suffering. The second epistle (2 Peter) refutes false teachings and explains the coming "day of the Lord."

Several non-biblical writers tell us that Peter was like Christ in that he was persecuted by religious leaders to the point of death. Church tradition says that in response to his objections not to be crucified in the same manner as Jesus, his executioners crucified him upside down.

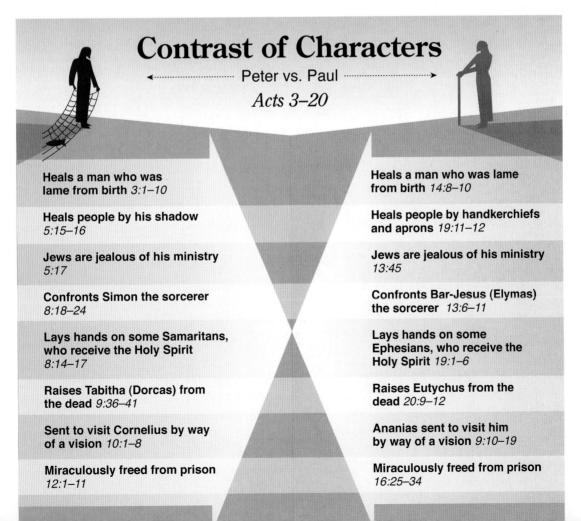

Contrast of Characters
— Peter vs. Paul —
Acts 3–20

Peter	Paul
Heals a man who was lame from birth 3:1–10	Heals a man who was lame from birth 14:8–10
Heals people by his shadow 5:15–16	Heals people by handkerchiefs and aprons 19:11–12
Jews are jealous of his ministry 5:17	Jews are jealous of his ministry 13:45
Confronts Simon the sorcerer 8:18–24	Confronts Bar-Jesus (Elymas) the sorcerer 13:6–11
Lays hands on some Samaritans, who receive the Holy Spirit 8:14–17	Lays hands on some Ephesians, who receive the Holy Spirit 19:1–6
Raises Tabitha (Dorcas) from the dead 9:36–41	Raises Eutychus from the dead 20:9–12
Sent to visit Cornelius by way of a vision 10:1–8	Ananias sent to visit him by way of a vision 9:10–19
Miraculously freed from prison 12:1–11	Miraculously freed from prison 16:25–34

PAUL (SAUL)

Paul's life displays God's ability to transform a person from a persecutor of the church to one of its most effective missionaries. Paul's ministry spans many years, geographically covering almost the entire Roman Empire, and 13 books of the New Testament (Romans, 1 and 2 Corinthians, Galatians, Ephesians, Philippians, Colossians, 1 and 2 Thessalonians, Philemon, Titus, and 1 and 2 Timothy) are attributed to Paul.

Paul, known as Saul before his repentance, is born in Tarsus (Acts 22:3), an important city in the Roman Empire. Paul is thoroughly Jewish, but his birthplace affords him the privileges of Roman citizenship, something he later uses to his advantage in sharing the gospel (Acts 16:12–40; 22:24–29; 23:23–24; 25:11–12).

As a young man, Paul is actively involved in persecuting the early church and imprisoning Christians for their faith (Acts 8:3; 9:1–2; Philippians 3:6). He is present and complicit when the first Christian martyr, Stephen, is stoned to death (Acts 7:58). As a member of the conservative Pharisee sect of Jews (Acts 23:6; Philippians 3:5), Paul attains a high level of theological education studying under Gamaliel, a well-known rabbi (Acts 22:3).

As Paul travels to the city of Damascus to arrest Christians, a light from heaven flashes around him. He hears a voice from heaven ask, "Saul, why do you persecute me?" This encounter with Christ leaves Paul blinded. When a Christian named Ananias prays for Paul, his sight is restored. Paul is

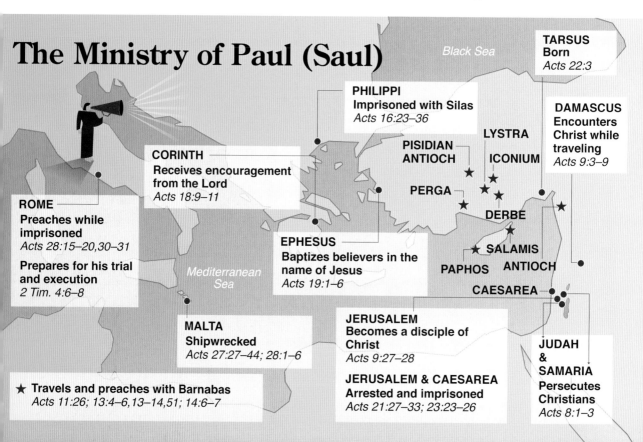

The Ministry of Paul (Saul)

TARSUS
Born
Acts 22:3

PHILIPPI
Imprisoned with Silas
Acts 16:23–36

DAMASCUS
Encounters
Christ while
traveling
Acts 9:3–9

LYSTRA
ICONIUM
PISIDIAN ANTIOCH
PERGA
DERBE

CORINTH
Receives encouragement
from the Lord
Acts 18:9–11

ROME
Preaches while
imprisoned
Acts 28:15–20,30–31

Prepares for his trial
and execution
2 Tim. 4:6–8

EPHESUS
Baptizes believers in the
name of Jesus
Acts 19:1–6

SALAMIS
PAPHOS ANTIOCH
CAESAREA

MALTA
Shipwrecked
Acts 27:27–44; 28:1–6

JERUSALEM
Becomes a disciple of
Christ
Acts 9:27–28

JUDAH
&
SAMARIA
Persecutes
Christians
Acts 8:1–3

JERUSALEM & CAESAREA
Arrested and imprisoned
Acts 21:27–33; 23:23–26

★ Travels and preaches with Barnabas
Acts 11:26; 13:4–6,13–14,51; 14:6–7

then baptized and spends time with the disciples in Damascus (Acts 9:2–19).

Shortly after his repentance, Paul goes to the desert area of Arabia and returns to Damascus (Galatians 1:15–20). He spends three years there before returning to the cities of Asia Minor. Paul's bold preaching and his repentance from persecuting Christians becomes widely known in the region, making him a target for church persecutors. A group of Jews attempts to kill him in Damascus (Acts 9:23–25), causing him to flee to Jerusalem.

When Paul arrives in Jerusalem, many Christians fear and do not trust him. Then Barnabas, a well-respected disciple who would later accompany Paul on his first mission, meets Paul and convinces the church that his repentance is genuine (Acts 9:27).

Paul goes on to become the greatest missionary of the early church. He takes four missionary journeys, founding, establishing, and teaching churches throughout the Roman Empire. As such, he becomes the apostle to the Gentiles, or the non-Jews. His letters instructing, correcting, and encouraging these churches and the leaders he appoints over them comprise a large percentage of the New Testament.

Paul endures many hardships during his ministry. He is persecuted, stoned, arrested, beaten, shipwrecked, and imprisoned. He preaches the gospel both when he is free and when he is imprisoned. He is ultimately sent to Rome, where, according to church tradition, he is executed by beheading because of his faith in Jesus Christ.

A Difficult Life

2 Corinthians 6:4–10; 11:23—12:10

Jesus once told Paul that he would suffer greatly for his faith, and 2 Corinthians recounts many of those difficulties

Number of Verses:

1 Persecution/ Hardship *12:10*

2 Imprisonment *6:5; 11:23*

3 Lack of basic needs *6:5,10; 11:27*

4 Danger *6:5; 11:23–26*

5 Personal difficulties *6:5,8; 11:28; 12:7*

6 Beatings/ Physical injury *6:5,9; 11:23–25*

© Zondervan. Used by permission

SUPPORTERS OF THE EARLY CHURCH

The years that immediately follow Jesus' death and resurrection are filled with many interesting followers of "the Way," the original term for followers of Christ (Acts 9:1–2). The modern church owes its heritage to these leaders who gave much to fulfill the mission Jesus left: the proclamation of God's kingdom (Luke 4:18–19). Without their dedication to spreading the Word, recording the history of Jesus' life, and preserving the many letters sent to the early churches throughout the known world, the church today would lack much of its rich history.

After Paul repents from being a persecutor of the early church and becomes a follower of the Way, many Christians in Jerusalem are still afraid of him. Barnabas, whose name means "son of encouragement," convinces people that Paul's repentance is

Apostles, Disciples and Supporters of the Early Church

ANANIAS

Obeys the law; receives respect from Jews
Acts 22:12

Lives in Damascus, where the Lord speaks to him
Acts 9:10–11

Sent by the Lord to see Saul
Acts 9:13–18

ANANIAS & SAPPHIRA

Sell property to benefit those in need
Acts 4:32–35; 5:1

Hold back some of the money they have pledged
Acts 5:2

Ananias dies after being confronted by Peter
Acts 5:3–5

Sapphira dies after lying about the price of the property
Acts 5:7–10

AQUILA & PRISCILLA

Work as tentmakers in Corinth
Acts 18:2–3

Move to Ephesus and teach about Jesus
Acts 18:18–19,25–26

Partner with Paul in ministry
Rom. 16:3–4

Open their home as a church
1 Cor. 16:19

EPAPHRODITUS

Sent by the church at Philippi to bring gifts to Paul
Phil. 4:18

Helps Paul while he is imprisoned in Rome
Phil. 2:25

Returns to Philippi because of illness
Phil. 2:26–30

APOLLOS

Born in Alexandria and moves to Ephesus
Acts 18:24

Taught by Aquila and Priscilla
Acts 18:25–26

Travels to Greece and helps the believers
Acts 18:27–28

genuine (Acts 9:26–27), enabling Paul to expand his ministry with the blessing of the apostles. Barnabas and his cousin Mark (Colossians 4:10) then accompany Paul on the first of his three missionary journeys.

Other important people in the early church include Stephen, the first martyr (Acts 6–7); Phoebe, a deaconess in the Cenchreae church who delivers Paul's epistle to the Romans (Romans 16:1–2); Apollos, who helps the disciples in their work among the Greeks (Acts 18:24–28); and Aquila and Priscilla, a husband and wife team who hear Apollos preach in the synagogue, invite him to their home, and explain "to him the way of God more adequately" (Acts 18:26). Without such people, the Christian church would not exist today.

BARNABAS

Originally named Joseph; is a Levite from Cyprus
Acts 4:36

Related to the apostle Mark (cousins)
Col. 4:10

Sells land and gives the money to the apostles
Acts 4:37

Brings Saul to the apostles when everyone rejects him
Acts 9:26–27

Filled with the Holy Spirit
Acts 11:24

Travels and preaches with Paul
Acts 12–15

AGABUS

Serves as a prophet
Acts 11:27; 21:10

Travels from Jerusalem to Antioch
Acts 11:27

Through the Spirit, predicts a famine
Acts 11:28–29

Travels from Judea to Caesarea
Acts 21:10

Prophesies Paul's arrest in Jerusalem
Acts 21:11

SILAS

Serves as a prophet and leader among the believers
Acts 15:22,32

Travels and preaches with Paul
Acts 16–17

Imprisoned with Paul
Acts 16:23–36

Delivers Peter's first epistle to church elders
1 Pet. 5:12

STEPHEN

Filled with faith and the Holy Spirit
Acts 6:5

Taken before the Sanhedrin on false charges
Acts 6:9–15

Speaks in his own defense
Acts 7:1–53

Stoned to death
Acts 7:55–60

PHOEBE

Serves as a deacon in the church at Cenchreae
Rom. 16:1

Highly esteemed by Paul
Rom. 16:1

Financially supports Paul and other believers
Rom. 16:2

Delivers Paul's epistle to the church in Rome
Rom. 16:2

JESUS' DISCIPLES

At the beginning of his ministry, Jesus calls 12 people to follow him and learn from him (Luke 6:12–16). He gives these disciples, or followers, authority over disease and demons and sends them out to proclaim the kingdom of heaven (Matthew 10:1–7).

From the beginning, Jesus warns his 12 disciples that they will suffer persecution (Matthew 10:16–42). He teaches that accepting his apostles is the same as accepting him (Matthew 10:40–42).

Church tradition and church history report that from among the original 12 apostles, only John dies of natural causes. Judas Iscariot betrays Jesus for 30 pieces of silver, then hangs himself (Matthew 27:3–8). The other apostles, along with Matthias, who is chosen as Judas's replacement, are martyred or killed for their faith.

Between AD 40 and 44, James, the brother of the apostle John, becomes the first apostle martyred. Herod Agrippa I orders him to be put to death (Acts 12:2), then arrests and persecutes other Christians after James's public execution meets with public approval. James's martyrdom is the only death of an apostle (other than Judas) recorded in Scripture.

Church tradition teaches that after Jesus' death, Philip preaches in the area known today as central Turkey. He is martyred by crucifixion. Some accounts suggest he is crucified head down in Hierapolis, near modern Pamukkale, Turkey, in AD 54.

According to tradition, James "the younger" is the next apostle martyred. He is thrown from the top of the temple in Jerusalem and beaten to death by an angry mob in AD 63.

Early in his ministry, Peter, "the rock," is imprisoned because of his faith (Acts 4:1–4). The Jewish rulers threaten him, demanding that he stop preaching in Jesus' name. Peter insists that he must obey God rather than men. In addition to preaching and performing miracles in Jesus' name, two epistles, or letters to the early church, are attributed to Peter. Tradition teaches that he is ultimately crucified—upside down, at his request because he did not feel worthy to be crucified in the same manner as Jesus—in Rome in AD 64.

Matthew, the former tax collector, ministers in Persia and Ethiopia after Jesus' resurrection. At some point during his ministry, he writes the Bible book of Matthew, an account of Jesus' life and ministry. Church history and tradition suggests that Matthew is beheaded sometime between AD 60 and 70 in Ethiopia.

Church history also tells us that four apostles die martyrs' deaths in AD 70. Andrew, Peter's brother, is hung from a tree in Patras. Thomas preaches in places as far off as China before being burned alive in India. Matthias serves as an evangelist in Armenia before being stoned to death while he is being crucified. Bartholomew travels and ministers throughout Asia Minor until he is crucified near the Caspian Sea.

The apostle Judas (not to be confused with Judas Iscariot) is also called Thaddaeus. He travels and preaches the gospel in Syria, Persia, and Armenia. He is ultimately beaten to death in Syria in AD 72. Simon "the zealot" travels and ministers in places ranging from Northern Africa to the British Isles before being crucified in Syria in AD 74.

John, called "the disciple whom Jesus loved" (John 13:23; 20:2; 21:7, 20), is the sole apostle to die a natural death, according to church tradition. He ministers in Jerusalem and later becomes the leader of the church in Ephesus. He is eventually exiled as a political prisoner to the Isle of Patmos, where he receives a series of visions from Jesus Christ that becomes the book of Revelation. Three epistles and one Gospel are also attributed to the apostle John — the Bible book of John and 1, 2, and 3 John.

CHAPTER 3

QUICKSCAN
BIBLE PLACES

THE LAND OF ISRAEL

Situated atop part of the Syrian-African rift, the land of Israel features a wide variety of natural landscapes within a relatively small geographic location. Ranging from mountains to deserts to fertile valleys, the entire land of Israel takes up less space than Lake Michigan in the United States of America.

Most of the land contains a climate similar to that of the Mediterranean region, experiencing hot, lengthy summers and cool, short winter seasons. The climate does vary significantly from region to region due to elevation, precipitation, and other natural phenomena. Temperatures in the land of Israel fluctuate between 82.4 degrees Fahrenheit in the hottest month of August to 41 degrees Fahrenheit during January, the country's coldest month.

The Negev Desert dominates the southern half of the land of Israel, covering over 6,000 square miles. This portion of the country sees very little precipitation, roughly four inches per year, most of which falls from October to April. The desert also features numerous freshwater springs, where water comes to the surface through limestone deposits.

The northern expanse of the Negev region in central Israel includes the Judean Desert, which encompasses the Dead Sea. To the west of the Dead Sea lie the Judean Hills, which function as useful terrain for raising sheep and other livestock. The hills give way to a flat, fertile plain as they approach the great Mediterranean Sea.

Many crops were grown in the fertile areas of Israel during biblical times, includ-

The Land of Israel

Most of the harvests were collected in spring and summer

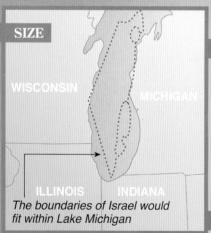

SIZE

WISCONSIN

MICHIGAN

ILLINOIS   INDIANA

The boundaries of Israel would fit within Lake Michigan

CROPS/NATURAL RESOURCES

There were many crops grown in ancient Israel, including

Barley, Wheat, Olives, Figs, Grapes, Pomegranates, Honey

Salt in ancient Israel was mined from the region around the Dead Sea

WATER

October – April
Wet season

Northern portion
(40 inches/1,000mm annually)

Southern portion
(4 inches/100mm annually)

Most of the water in the desert came from springs that would come up through the limestone

The areas along the coastline would experience heavy dew in the morning

CLIMATE*

January—the coldest month

41°F (5°C)

82.4°F (28°C)

August—the hottest month

*Average temperatures

ing barley, wheat, olives, figs, grapes, and pomegranates (Deuteronomy 8:8). In the autumn, planting for barley and wheat begins along with olive harvesting. By spring, these grains are ready to be harvested, while dates, figs, grapes, and pomegranates are harvested in summer. Today, Israeli agriculture makes the country virtually self-sufficient for the people's food needs. While many of the historical items are still grown, today's agricultural industry is also known for its vegetables and citrus fruits.

The Dead Sea, a geographic wonder, takes in water from several rivers, most notably the Jordan River. The Jordan flows south from the Sea of Galilee, descending rapidly into the mouth of the Dead Sea, the lowest elevation point on earth. No water flows out of the Dead Sea. This fact, along with the high temperatures in the region, creates the saltiest water with the highest mineral content in the world. The water is so heavily saline that no marine life can be sustained within it. For this reason, the Israelites used the Dead Sea as a mine for salt.

The northern half of Israel receives considerably more rainfall than the southern half, averaging 40 inches per year. It also contains the Carmel mountain range, with the Jezreel Valley—one of the most fertile regions in the Middle East—to its east. The Jezreel Valley gives way to the hilly Galilean region, which includes the Sea of Galilee, a large inland lake subject to sudden

and violent storms. To the east of the Sea of Galilee is the Bashan region, with snow-capped mountains, including Mt. Hermon. Today, this entire region is referred to as the Golan Heights.

During much of the biblical period, the land of Israel featured only two major roads: the Way of the Sea along the Mediterranean Coast, and the King's Highway, running north to south in the western portion of Israel. Several other widely used but beaten-down paths connect the major geographical regions and towns. None of the region's roads were paved until the land came under the control of the Roman Empire many years later.

The 12 Tribes of Israel

ASHER NAPHTALI EAST MANASSEH

ZEBULUN

ISSACHAR

MANASSEH

GAD

EPHRAIM

DAN

BENJAMIN

JUDAH

REUBEN

Dead Sea

SIMEON

DEAD SEA

The Dead Sea is an inland lake in the Jordan River Valley whose shores include the lowest surface elevation on earth. The lake takes in water from the Jordan River, the Arnon Gorge, and small tributaries and springs, but no water flows out of it. This, combined with the area's heat and high rate of evaporation, causes the lake to be ten times saltier than the world's oceans. Because of this, no marine life can survive in its waters.

The Bible refers to the Dead Sea as the Sea of Arabah (Deuteronomy 3:17). Different Bible translations refer to the Dead Sea as the east sea, the sea of the plain, the sea of the wilderness, and the Salt Sea. During the days of ancient Israel, the Dead Sea formed part of the nation's southeastern border. This fact is noted in several Biblical accounts.

The cities of Sodom and Gomorrah may have been situated on or near the shore of the Dead Sea. Sodom and Gomorrah were made infamous for their inhabitants' wickedness and sexual perversion and were eventually destroyed by the Lord (Genesis 19:25).

Approximately 400 years after the destruction of these cities, one million Israelites prepare to cross the Jordan in order to enter the Promised Land (Joshua 3). They have been living as nomads in the wilderness for 40 years.

After another 400 years, the land west of the Dead Sea, also known as En Gedi, becomes a safe haven for the young David (1 Samuel 23:29).

Ezekiel 47:8–9 and Zechariah 14:8 refer to freshwater entering the Dead Sea, making it able to sustain life once more. Scholars debate the interpretation of the language in this prophecy: it could be figurative or it could describe a reality that will one day materialize after the return of Christ.

Dead Sea

●JERUSALEM

Living water will flow from the temple in Jerusalem to the Dead Sea
Zech. 14:8

Jordan River

Dead Sea

Water stops flowing to the Dead Sea so God's people can cross the Jordan River
Josh. 3:15–16

King Jeroboam restores Israel's eastern border back to the Dead Sea
2 Kings 14:23–25

God protects his people from invaders
Joel 2:20

Eastern border of Israel
Num. 34:3–12

SEA OF GALILEE

The Sea of Galilee is a freshwater lake surrounded by the mountainous terrain of northeastern Israel. Its shores include some of the most fertile land in the Upper Jordan region. The lake is known for its sudden, violent storms, caused by powerful winds from the mountains clashing with the lake's warm surface temperature. The lake is also referred to as the Sea of Kinnereth (Old Testament), the Lake of Gennesaret (Luke 5:1), and the Sea of Tiberias (John 6:1; 21:1).

The Sea of Galilee comes into greater prominence in the New Testament. It is here where Jesus begins to preach and where he is first recorded saying, "Repent, for the kingdom of heaven has come near" (Matthew 4:17). Jesus is walking along the Sea of Galilee's shoreline when he calls Andrew and Peter, his first disciples. They are fishing in the lake and leave their nets on its shores when Jesus beckons. Jesus also calls James and John to follow him while they are on their father's boat on the lake (Matthew 4:21–22). In all, 11 of Jesus' 12 disciples come from the area near the Sea of Galilee.

The Sea of Galilee functions as a type of "home base" for much of Jesus' teaching ministry. He also performs many of his miracles near the Sea of Galilee: he amazes his disciples by calming one of the lake's violent storms (Mark 4:35–41); he miraculously feeds thousands of people with five loaves of bread and a few fish (John 6:1–15); he walks on the water (John 6:16–21); he instructs Peter to catch a fish that contains a four-drachma coin in its mouth (Matthew 17:24–27); and he heals many people near the lake's shores.

After Jesus is crucified and resurrected, his disciples return to the area where most of them lived before following Jesus. One night, they go fishing on the Sea of Galilee. They fish all night without catching anything. Then they hear Jesus call out to them from the shore, "Friends, haven't you any fish?" (John 21:5). They don't recognize him at first and answer no. Jesus tells them, "Throw your net on the right side of the boat and you will find some" (John 21:6a). When their nets become so heavy that they cannot haul them in, the disciples realize that the man on the shore is Jesus, raised from the dead (John 21:6b–7).

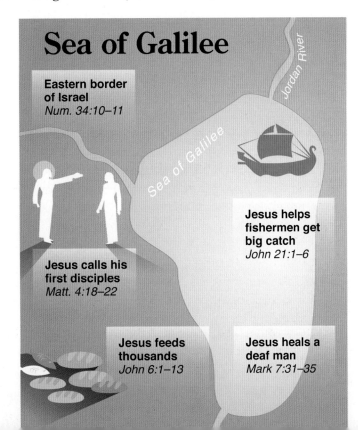

Sea of Galilee

Eastern border
of Israel
Num. 34:10–11

Sea of Galilee

Jordan River

**Jesus helps
fishermen get
big catch**
John 21:1–6

**Jesus calls his
first disciples**
Matt. 4:18–22

**Jesus feeds
thousands**
John 6:1–13

**Jesus heals a
deaf man**
Mark 7:31–35

JORDAN RIVER

The Jordan River, which plays a significant role in both the Old and New Testaments, spans over 100 miles, starting at Mount Hermon and flowing between the Sea of Galilee in northern Israel and the Dead Sea. This fast-moving river flows from an elevation of 1,200 feet above sea level to a dramatic 1,286 feet below sea level at the rate of 25 feet per mile.

The Jordan River first enters the biblical narrative in Genesis 13. Abram (Abraham) and his nephew Lot part ways after they both experience increasing prosperity—the land is not big enough for their families' combined animals and possessions. Lot decides to move his family and flocks east to the area of Sodom, one of five wicked cities situated within the well-watered Jordan plain (Genesis 13:10), while Abram moves his family to a region located between the Dead Sea and the Mediterranean Sea (known as Hebron).

Decades later, Abraham's grandson Jacob crosses over the Jordan River when he flees from his brother, Esau (Genesis 27:41–28:5), and again when he returns to the land of Canaan with his family. Jacob is near the river when he prays to God for protection from his vengeful brother (Genesis 32:9–12). The ford of the Jabbok, which flows into the Jordan River, is the location of Jacob's famous wrestling match with God (Genesis 32:22–30). Here, God changes Jacob's name to Israel, meaning, "He struggles with God."

More than 400 years later, after the people of Israel (the descendants of Jacob) endure slavery and traveling through the desert, they find themselves at the Jordan. They set up camp on the east side of the river and stay there for some time. The Israelites listen to Moses along the river's shores. He explains God's law to them, preparing them to live faithfully in the Promised Land (Numbers 33:50–35:34). However, because Moses disobeyed God at one point in the desert, God does not grant him permission to lead the people into the land (Deuteronomy 32:48–52). This will be a privilege that his successor, Joshua, will experience years later (Deuteronomy 3:21–29).

The Jordan River is at flood stage when Joshua, Israel's new leader, assembles and instructs the people to consecrate them-

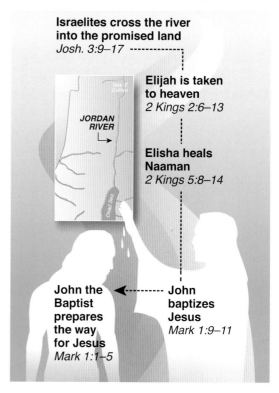

Jordan River

Israelites cross the river into the promised land
Josh. 3:9–17

JORDAN RIVER

Elijah is taken to heaven
2 Kings 2:6–13

Elisha heals Naaman
2 Kings 5:8–14

John the Baptist prepares the way for Jesus
Mark 1:1–5

John baptizes Jesus
Mark 1:9–11

selves to the Lord (Joshua 3:5–15). He tells them that they will know God is among them when they witness the waters of the Jordan standing "in a heap" (Joshua 3:16) on either side. God shows his people that it is his power alone that enables them to cross over into the land he is giving to them. After crossing the Jordan, the Israelites take 12 stones, one for each tribe of Israel, from the Jordan's riverbed and set them up as a memorial so that future generations will know that God parted the waters again for his people (Joshua 4:1–9).

After the crossing, the Israelite tribes of Gad and Reuben and the half-tribe of Manasseh remain in the land east of the Jordan River, while the remaining tribes settle on the other side.

While the land surrounding the Jordan is the Promised Land for God's people, it is also a place of continued battle. The Israelites face many invading forces there. During the time of the judges, the Ammonites, Midianites, and Philistines cross over the river in order to attack Israel.

Beyond being a place of rest and battle, the land surrounding the Jordan is also a place of significance for God's prophets. Both Elijah and Elisha, two of Israel's greatest prophets, conduct much of their ministry near the Jordan. Here, God grants Elisha, Elijah's successor, a "double portion" of Elijah's spirit after Elijah is taken directly to heaven without dying (2 Kings 2:7–12). At one point, Elisha strikes the water with Elijah's cloak in order to part the river so that he can cross over on dry ground (2 Kings 2:13–14). Soon after, Naaman, a high-ranking military general from the enemy nation of Syria, visits Elisha. He seeks out Elisha for healing after hearing of God's power at work in the prophet's life. Elisha instructs the general to bathe in the Jordan River. After Naaman dips in the water seven times, God heals him of leprosy (2 Kings 5:8–14).

Many years later, John the Baptist travels around the area of the Jordan River and preaches a message of repentance in order to prepare people's hearts for the coming of Jesus (Luke 3:3–6). John baptizes Jesus the Messiah (Mark 1:9–11) in the Jordan River. As Jesus emerges from the water, the heavens are torn open and the Holy Spirit descends on Jesus like a dove. The voice of God from heaven declares, "You are my Son, whom I love; with you I am well pleased" (Mark 1:11).

Today, the Jordan River serves as the border between the nation of Israel and the Kingdom of Jordan.

JERICHO

Jericho is a city located near the Jordan River, to the north of the Dead Sea, roughly 17 miles to the northeast of Jerusalem. Over the years, the city has occupied at least three distinct sites, and it is now one of the oldest continuously occupied cities in the world.

Jericho is located in the midst of an oasis and is often referred to as the "City of Palms" (Judges 3:13). It is situated near the nadir of a deep gorge 800 feet below sea level, giving it the lowest elevation of any city on earth.

The Israelites camped across the Jordan River from the ancient city of Jericho just before entering the Promised Land. They were within a few miles of the city when God told Moses that he had given the land of Canaan to the Israelites and that they were to drive out all of the inhabitants and destroy all of the idols in the land (Numbers 33:50–56).

After Moses had died, Joshua sent a pair of spies into Canaan with instructions to look over the land, "especially Jericho" (Joshua 2:1). The city was surrounded by massive walls at the time.

Jericho

The Lord gives Jericho and the surrounding land to the Israelites
Num. 33:50–53

Joshua sends spies to Jericho who are saved by a prostitute named Rahab
Josh. 2:1, 14–16

Israelites destroy Jericho
Josh. 6:20–21

JERICHO •

Dead Sea

Joshua proclaims a curse on anyone who attempts to rebuild Jericho
Josh. 6:26

Jesus heals a blind man
Mark 10:46–52

Zacchaeus meets Jesus
Luke 19:1–10

In the city, a prostitute named Rahab protected the spies by hiding them and helping them escape when the king of Jericho was looking for them. She made them promise that, in return, they would spare her and her family when the Israelites conquered Jericho (Joshua 2). Ultimately, Rahab was not only saved, but became a direct ancestor of King David and Jesus (Matthew 1:5).

Jericho is the first city conquered by the Israelites after they cross the Jordan River into the Promised Land. People from Jericho certainly noticed the large gathering of Israelites camped across the river. Joshua 6 tells us that the city's gates were "securely barred" and that no one was allowed in or out because of the approaching Israelites (Joshua 6:1).

Those inside the city would

have seen the Israelite fighting men marching around the city, following priests carrying trumpets made out of rams' horns and the ark of the covenant. After seven days of marching, the Israelites shouted and blew the trumpets, and the city's walls collapsed.

After the Israelites overran Jericho, Joshua pronounced a curse on anyone rebuilding the city (Joshua 6:26). This curse was fulfilled over 500 years later, during the reign of Ahab. The man who rebuilt Jericho —Hiel of Bethel—lost two sons in the process (1 Kings 16:34).

Shortly after that time, there was a company of prophets at Jericho. Elijah and Elisha spent time there. Fifty of Jericho's prophets watched as the Jordan River parted when Elijah struck it with his cloak (2 Kings 2:7–8).

Jericho also played a role in the New Testament. Most scholars believe the location of the city of Jericho mentioned in the Gospels was a couple of miles south of the site of the fortress city the Israelites conquered under Joshua.

Jesus mentions the road to Jericho in the parable of the Good Samaritan (Luke 10:30–37). The rough, hilly terrain the road passed through was ideal for bandits and highwaymen like those in Jesus' story.

Jesus visits Jericho on at least two occasions. A person in the city at the time would have noticed the crowd following Jesus. He or she might have been distracted by the blind beggar hollering, "Jesus, Son of David, have mercy on me!" Such a person might have even witnessed Jesus restoring Bartimaeus's sight (Mark 10:46–52).

During another of Jesus' visits to Jericho, a person living there might have noticed Zacchaeus—a hated tax collector —climbing a fig tree to get a look at Jesus. A resident might have heard Jesus call the man out of the tree and invite himself to dinner at the tax collector's home. Most of Jericho's inhabitants likely heard about Zacchaeus's offer to repay four times the amount he had cheated people of. A person in the crowd that day could have even listened as Jesus told the parable of the ten minas (Luke 19:11–27).

JERUSALEM

Jerusalem, the most significant city in the Bible, serves as the backdrop for many events in the Old and New Testaments.

Jerusalem is first mentioned during the Israelites' conquest of Canaan, or the Promised Land. The king of Jerusalem is nervous about Joshua's conquests in the area, so he forms an alliance with four neighboring kings in order to attack Gibeon, a nation that recently made a peace treaty with Israel. The Israelites end up annihilating Jerusalem's army and killing its king (Joshua 10).

During the period of the judges, the people of Judah capture the king of Jerusalem, then attack the city (Judges 1:8). A Canaanite tribe, the Jebusites, later rebuilds Jerusalem as a fortified city.

During the reign of King David, the Israelites conquer Jerusalem, making it their capital, likely because of the city's significant natural defenses (2 Samuel 5:6–10). David's son, Solomon, eventually builds the Lord's temple in Jerusalem, making the city the religious epicenter for God's people (1 Kings 6:37–38). During holy days, faithful Israelites are expected to make regular pilgrimages to worship and offer sacrifices in Jerusalem.

During the period of Israel's monarchy, when the Hebrews are divided into northern (Israel) and southern kingdoms (Judah), Jerusalem remains Judah's capital. Many enemies, including the Egyptians and Assyrians, attack Jerusalem several times. Those living in the city witness God miraculously saving the people of Jerusalem. However, God eventually allows the city and its temple to be destroyed by the Babylonians, who send the Israelites into exile.

For seventy years, only the poorest of God's people remain in Jerusalem until God uses Cyrus, a Persian emperor, to conquer the Babylonian Empire. Cyrus frees the Jewish exiles to return to Jerusalem in two large waves, the first under the priest Zerubbabel, to rebuild the temple, and the second under Nehemiah, to rebuild the walls of the city (Nehemiah mobilizes different family groups to rebuild each section of the wall). The prophet Ezra leads a covenant revival and a renewal of the Israelites' commitment to the law of Moses.

By the time Jesus is born, Jerusalem is under the rule of the Roman Empire but remains the center of the Jewish culture. Mary and Joseph, Jesus' human parents, present him for circumcision in the temple in Jerusalem. When Jesus is a young child, he travels to Jerusalem with his family to celebrate holy days.

Later in Jesus' ministry, Jerusalem is the backdrop for significant events such as his encounter with the woman caught in adultery (John 8:1–11), "cleansing" the temple (Matthew 21:12–17), the Last Supper, and, finally, Jesus' arrest, crucifixion, and resurrection.

Jerusalem continues to be significant to the early church. It is in Jerusalem that believers are first filled with the Holy Spirit on the Day of Pentecost (Acts 2), and the administration of the early church throughout the Roman Empire is centered in Jerusalem (Acts 15). Finally, the new Jerusalem is described in Revelation as the city of God, the holy city, "coming down out of heaven from God," when God restores heaven and earth (Revelation 21:2; 21:10).

Walls and Their Builders

Nehemiah 3 tells us the names of many who help rebuild Jerusalem's wall

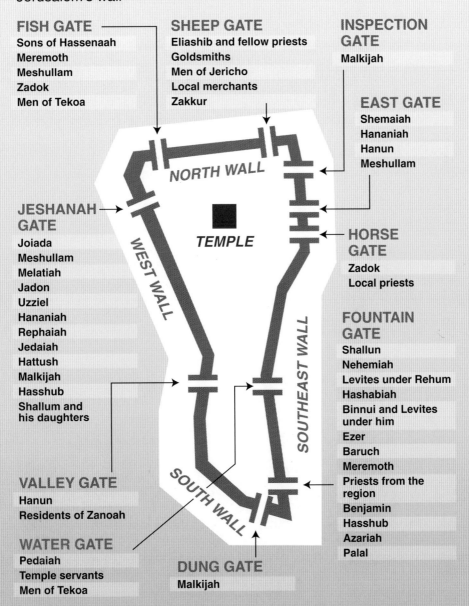

FISH GATE
Sons of Hassenaah
Meremoth
Meshullam
Zadok
Men of Tekoa

SHEEP GATE
Eliashib and fellow priests
Goldsmiths
Men of Jericho
Local merchants
Zakkur

INSPECTION GATE
Malkijah

EAST GATE
Shemaiah
Hananiah
Hanun
Meshullam

JESHANAH GATE
Joiada
Meshullam
Melatiah
Jadon
Uzziel
Hananiah
Rephaiah
Jedaiah
Hattush
Malkijah
Hasshub
Shallum and his daughters

HORSE GATE
Zadok
Local priests

FOUNTAIN GATE
Shallun
Nehemiah
Levites under Rehum
Hashabiah
Binnui and Levites under him
Ezer
Baruch
Meremoth
Priests from the region
Benjamin
Hasshub
Azariah
Palal

VALLEY GATE
Hanun
Residents of Zanoah

WATER GATE
Pedaiah
Temple servants
Men of Tekoa

DUNG GATE
Malkijah

NORTH WALL
WEST WALL
TEMPLE
SOUTHEAST WALL
SOUTH WALL

THE TABERNACLE

After their deliverance from Egypt, the Israelites wander in the desert for 40 years. Needing a physical structure in which to give sacrifices and offerings, the Israelites are instructed by God to construct a tabernacle. God intends the tabernacle, or the "tent of meeting," to be a portable place of worship (Exodus 35–38).

The tabernacle frame is made from acacia wood overlaid in gold, while the frame's cover is made of rams' skins (Exodus 36:19–34). Inside, curtains divide the tabernacle into an outer and inner tent. The outer tent is made with 11 curtains of goat hair, while the inner tent is made with ten curtains of fine linen yarn (Exodus 36:8–18).

Any Israelite can enter the tabernacle courtyard, but only priests can enter into the tabernacle structure itself. Only the high priest can enter into the inner tent, the Holy of Holies, where God's presence dwells. The high priest can enter only once per year. He must always bring a blood sacrifice (Hebrews 9:7) in order to seek forgiveness for his sins and the sins of the people.

The outer tent contains a golden table that holds special bread as an offering to God, a lampstand, and an incense altar (Exodus 37:17–27).

The inner tent contains the ark of the covenant, a rectangular wooden chest containing the tablets of God's law, or the Ten Commandments; Aaron's staff; and a jar of the miraculous food God daily provided during Israel's time in the wilderness (manna) (Hebrews 9:4).

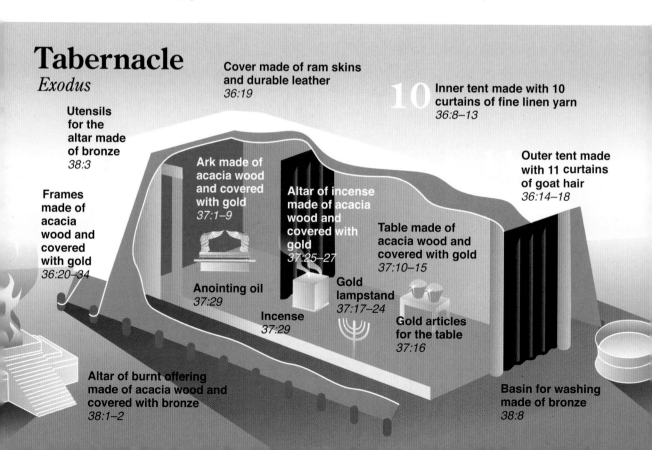

Tabernacle
Exodus

Cover made of ram skins and durable leather
36:19

10 Inner tent made with 10 curtains of fine linen yarn
36:8–13

Utensils for the altar made of bronze
38:3

Outer tent made with 11 curtains of goat hair
36:14–18

Frames made of acacia wood and covered with gold
36:20–34

Ark made of acacia wood and covered with gold
37:1–9

Altar of incense made of acacia wood and covered with gold
37:25–27

Table made of acacia wood and covered with gold
37:10–15

Anointing oil
37:29

Gold lampstand
37:17–24

Incense
37:29

Gold articles for the table
37:16

Altar of burnt offering made of acacia wood and covered with bronze
38:1–2

Basin for washing made of bronze
38:8

THE TEMPLE

The temple's main areas include the outer and inner courts, the Holy Place, and the Most Holy Place, also known as the Holy of Holies. In the inner courtyard sits a bronze altar for burnt offerings (1 Kings 8:22), and atop twelve bronze bulls sits an enormous bowl used by priests for ritual washings (1 Kings 7:25). A pair of ornate pillars marks the entrance into the Holy Place.

Inside the Holy Place is an altar for incense, a table for a special bread offering to God, ten lampstands, and utensils for use in animal sacrifices.

A massive veil separates the inner court from the Most Holy Place. Behind the veil sits the ark of the covenant, the sacred gold-plated box containing the tablets of the law, overshadowed by a pair of golden cherubim.

The first temple was built by Solomon and was destroyed in 586 BC. A second temple was built after the exile and completed in 515 BC. After standing five centuries, this smaller temple was rebuilt into a magnificent structure by Herod the Great and stood until AD 70, when it was destroyed by the Romans.

The Temple

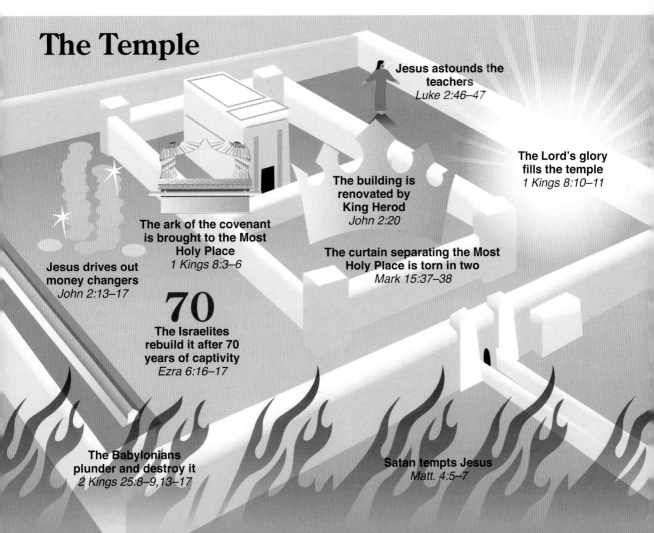

Jesus astounds the teachers
Luke 2:46–47

The Lord's glory fills the temple
1 Kings 8:10–11

The building is renovated by King Herod
John 2:20

The ark of the covenant is brought to the Most Holy Place
1 Kings 8:3–6

The curtain separating the Most Holy Place is torn in two
Mark 15:37–38

Jesus drives out money changers
John 2:13–17

70
The Israelites rebuild it after 70 years of captivity
Ezra 6:16–17

The Babylonians plunder and destroy it
2 Kings 25:8–9, 13–17

Satan tempts Jesus
Matt. 4:5–7

ASSYRIA

What the Bible refers to as Assyria is located in modern-day southeastern Turkey and northern Iraq. The Bible first mentions the land of Assyria in Genesis as a reference point for the location of the Tigris River, one of four rivers flowing from the Garden of Eden (Genesis 2:14; NIV: Ashur). While the nation of Assyria did not exist at that point in history, the fact that Moses uses it as a reference point later suggests that it exists by the time the Israelites are ready to enter the Promised Land.

Later in Hebrew history, Assyria is a kingdom in northern Mesopotamia that grows to become one of the greatest empires in the ancient Middle East. At the height of its power, the Assyrian Empire spreads from as far south as Egypt to as far west as Asia Minor. Assyria conquers most of this region, forcing other kingdoms to accept "client state" status under which they must pay tribute. In battle, the Assyrians have a reputation for savagery and cruelty toward the defeated. They typically loot and raze cities that oppose them. Stone carvings in their cities depict Assyrian soldiers blinding enemy warriors, torturing children, impaling people on stakes, and beheading their enemies.

At one point, the prophet Jonah visits the residents of Assyria's capital,

Nineveh. He calls them to repent, warning them of God's pending judgment. When the Ninevites repent and cry out to God for mercy, God spares them (Jonah 2:10 – 3:10). However, within a century of Jonah's visit, the Assyrians fall back into wickedness. During this time, Assyrians surround both Israel and Judah, posing a constant threat to both kingdoms. Nahum, an Israelite prophet, preaches against Assyria and foretells its fall from power (Nahum 3:18 – 19).

The Assyrians eventually conquer the northern kingdom of Israel and deport its residents (2 Kings 18:11 – 12). The northern kingdom never recovers. The Assyrians relocate people from other parts of their empire into Samaria, the former capital of Israel. This leads to animosity between Jews and Samaritans, a tension that continues into New Testament times (John 4:9).

The Assyrians also conquer much of the southern kingdom of Judah, destroying most of its fortified cities (Isaiah 36:1).

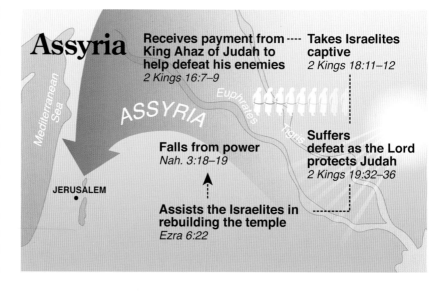

During this time, Isaiah prophesies the fall of the Assyrian Empire, while Jerusalem and Judah remain under God's protection. Later, the Assyrians fail to capture Jerusalem because of God's divine assistance (2 Kings 19).

Several other prophets also mention Assyria. Hosea foretells the northern kingdom's fall to Assyria (Hosea 11:5). Zephaniah foretells its fall from power (Zephaniah 2:13). Micah prophesies that God will deliver his people from Assyria (Micah 5:6). Jeremiah (2:36) and Ezekiel (31:3; 32:22) point back to the fall of Assyria after the prophecies of Isaiah and his contemporaries are fulfilled.

The people of Babylonia, which is a province of Assyria at this point, eventually break away from the Assyrian Empire and become the region's superpower. During this time, the people of Judah and Israel war against one another. This leads the king of Judah to ask the king of Assyria for protection. As a result, Judah becomes a "client kingdom," and its people are forced to send gold and silver from the temple to Assyria as a tribute (2 Kings 16:1–9).

Eventually, the Babylonians, under Nebuchadnezzar II, conquer both Assyria and Judah. This leads to the Babylonian Exile—the forced relocation of the southern kingdom's Israelites to Babylon. During the exile, the Persians, under Cyrus, conquer the Babylonians, bringing Assyria and Judah into the Persian Empire.

When Cyrus and his successors, Darius and Artaxerxes, allow the Jews and other captive peoples to return to their homelands, it causes conflict between Judah and other client kingdoms. During this time, God changes the attitude of the king of Assyria, and he assists the Israelites in rebuilding the temple (Ezra 6:22).

Throughout the periods of the Babylonian and Persian Empires, Assyria is absorbed into a series of conquering dynasties, yet it remains a distinct province. It becomes part of Alexander the Great's empire during the period between the Old and New Testaments.

During New Testament times, Assyria is part of the Parthian Empire. From 66 BC to AD 217, the Parthian Empire goes to war with the Roman Empire several times. During most of Jesus' lifetime, the people of both empires enjoy a season of uneasy peace. Assyria eventually becomes part of the Roman Empire in AD 116.

Today, some of the descendants of the Assyrian people continue to live as an Eastern Rite Christian minority in parts of Iran, Iraq, Turkey, and Syria.

BABYLON

The ancient city of Babylon is located on the Euphrates River about 59 miles southwest of present-day Baghdad, Iraq. In the Bible, Babylon is first mentioned in Genesis 10 as one of the early centers of Nimrod's kingdom (Genesis 10:9–10). The Babylonian legacy appears in the New Testament as a symbol of decadence and evil (Revelation 14; 17; 18).

In the Old Testament, Babylon plays a central role during Hezekiah's reign as king of Judah (approximately 700 BC). King Hezekiah boasts of his kingdom's riches to envoys from Babylonia, a relatively minor power at this time that is subject to the Assyrian Empire. This prompts the prophet Isaiah to foretell the rise of the Babylonian Empire and Judah's future captivity in Babylon (2 Kings 20:12–19; Isaiah 39:3–8). Although Isaiah prophesies the fall of Israel to the Babylonians, he also prophesies that Babylon will eventually be destroyed and turned into a wasteland (Isaiah 14:22–23).

When the Babylonian Empire rises to power, the city of Babylon becomes a center of learning and the arts. It houses the Hanging Gardens, a series of terraced gardens described as one of the most beautiful wonders of the ancient world by Greek and Roman writers. At the same time, Babylon also becomes a haven of immorality, which stems from its residents' religious practices, at least in the opinion of the Hebrew prophets. The Ishtar Gate, the most notable of the eight gates that ring the city, is dedicated to the goddess of fertility, alehouses, and prostitution. A large shrine is featured prominently in the city's temple area. A 40-foot golden image of Babylon's chief deity, Mar-

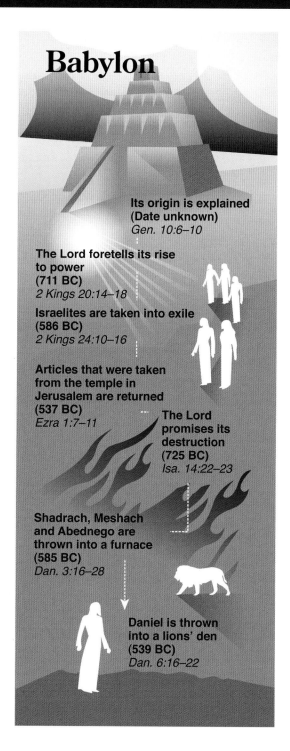

Babylon

Its origin is explained
(Date unknown)
Gen. 10:6–10

The Lord foretells its rise
to power
(711 BC)
2 Kings 20:14–18

Israelites are taken into exile
(586 BC)
2 Kings 24:10–16

Articles that were taken
from the temple in
Jerusalem are returned
(537 BC)
Ezra 1:7–11

The Lord
promises its
destruction
(725 BC)
Isa. 14:22–23

Shadrach, Meshach
and Abednego are
thrown into a furnace
(585 BC)
Dan. 3:16–28

Daniel is thrown
into a lions' den
(539 BC)
Dan. 6:16–22

duk, god of fertility and vegetation, sits atop the shrine. The Hebrews themselves are continually distracted by the Canaanite fertility gods, and the prophets of Yahweh preach that this is the primary reason for Israel's defeat and exile.

Isaiah's prophecy is fulfilled when the Babylonians invade Judah during the reign of Jehoiakim, Hezekiah's great-great-grandson. Over the next 20 years, the Babylonians take the people of Judah to Babylon in three waves of deportations (2 Kings 24:10–25:21). During this period, the Babylonians remove all articles of bronze, silver, and gold from the Lord's temple and place them in the temples of their gods.

Around the time of the Israelites' captivity, the Babylonian Empire reaches the height of its power. Babylon emerges as perhaps the largest city on earth, with an estimated population of over 200,000 people. An exiled Jew living in the capital at the time would witness great public works as they are being constructed. Many of the Jewish exiles are skilled craftsmen and are likely conscripted to work on the city's expansions (2 Kings 24:16).

During the first wave of captivity, the prophet Daniel is deported to Babylon along with his friends Shadrach, Meshach, and Abednego. While in captivity, Daniel rises to prominence in the Babylonian government, prophesies, and writes the largely apocalyptic book of the Bible that bears his name. Several years later, during the second wave of captivity, the prophet Ezekiel is deported and finishes the latter part of his ministry in Babylon. During this time, Jeru-salem is conquered, dashing the Israelites' hope of returning to their homeland.

During the exilic period, Babylonian king Nebuchadnezzar erects a giant golden statue and commands all "nations and peoples of every language" (Daniel 3:4) to worship the idol. When the sound of musical instruments fills the air, people are to bow down in worship. When Shadrach, Meshach, and Abednego refuse to bow down, they are sentenced to death in a fiery furnace. A man who looks "like a son of the gods" (Daniel 3:25) joins them in the fire, and they survive unharmed.

Sixty-six years after the start of the Babylonian captivity, the Persian Empire conquers Babylon—and inherits its exiles, including the Jews. Cyrus the Great, the Persian ruler, issues a decree called the Edict of Restoration, allowing the Jews and other exiles to return to their homelands. He also restores many of the gold and silver items that had been captured from the temple (Ezra 1). Under this decree, some Jews return to their homeland; however, many others choose to stay in Babylon, where they have established their lives and families.

Five to six centuries later (in the first century AD), a significant Jewish population still exists in Babylon. In his writing, Peter mentions a church in Babylon (1 Peter 5:13); however, he may not be referring to the actual city of Babylon. The New Testament writers often use the word *Babylon* symbolically to represent the sin and wickedness of the Roman Empire, especially religious corruption. Revelation 17:5 refers to Babylon as the "mother of prostitutes and of the abominations of the earth."

DAMASCUS

Damascus, located in modern-day Syria, is one of the oldest continually inhabited cities in the world. Throughout biblical history, Damascus often comes into conflict with Israel because of the city's strategic position along key trade routes.

In Genesis, when Abram goes to war to rescue his nephew Lot, he pursues Lot's captors to the area north of the city (Genesis 14:15).

Later, King David conquers Damascus after the city's warriors help his enemies. David places garrisons within the city, forcing the inhabitants to pay tribute (2 Samuel 8:5–6). Remnants of the army that David had defeated later reclaim Damascus. This occurs during King Solomon's reign, making Damascus Israel's adversary once again (1 Kings 11:23–25). Damascus then goes through several wars, again finding itself under the control of Israel, Aram, and other kingdoms throughout the years (2 Kings 14:8; 2 Kings 16:9).

Approximately one century after Damascus is recaptured from King Solomon, God sends Elijah into the desert that surrounds the city. There, Elijah meets Elisha, his successor, and anoints new kings over Aram and Israel (1 Kings 19:10–18). About 40 to 50 years later, the prophet Amos foretells the overthrow of Damascus and the captivity of its people (Amos 1:3–5). This prophecy is fulfilled when the Assyrians capture Damascus in 732 BC.

During New Testament times, Damascus is part of the province of Syria and the Decapolis, ten cities on the eastern frontier of the Roman Empire. After a long tradition of Greek and later Roman influence, the city has a tiny Jewish population. Nevertheless, Damascus is important to the development of Christianity.

The apostle Paul is on his way to Damascus to arrest Christians when he has a dramatic encounter with Jesus that leaves him blind. Once Paul arrives in Damascus, a Christian named Ananias receives a vision from God and seeks Paul out. Ananias prays for Paul, restoring his sight. Jews in the synagogues of Damascus become the first to hear Paul proclaim that Jesus is the Son of God (Acts 9).

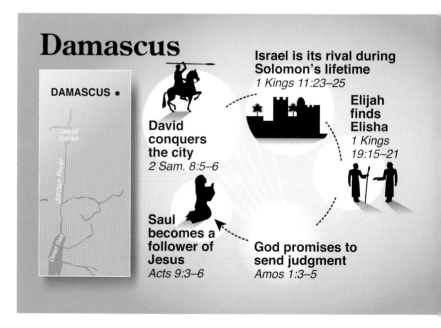

Damascus

DAMASCUS •

Sea of Galilee

Jordan River

Dead Sea

David conquers the city
2 Sam. 8:5–6

Saul becomes a follower of Jesus
Acts 9:3–6

Israel is its rival during Solomon's lifetime
1 Kings 11:23–25

Elijah finds Elisha
1 Kings 19:15–21

God promises to send judgment
Amos 1:3–5

EGYPT

Early in Scripture, Abram and Sarai escape famine in the land of Canaan by traveling south to Egypt (Genesis 12:10). There, God tells Abram (now called Abraham) that his descendants will be enslaved in this land for 400 years before they inherit the Promised Land (Genesis 15:13–14). This place of provision becomes a place of bondage, and Egypt later becomes a symbol for captivity throughout the Bible.

Jacob's youngest and favorite son, Joseph, is the first of Abraham's descendants to live in slavery. He is sold by his brothers to a traveling band of merchants (Genesis 37:12–36). Joseph remains faithful to God in Egypt, and despite being framed by Pharaoh's wife and forgotten by a fellow prisoner he helps, he eventually rises from his position as a slave to become the second-most powerful man in Egypt (Genesis 39–41).

When famine strikes in Canaan again, Joseph's brothers come to Egypt to buy grain. Joseph recognizes and shows mercy to his estranged family, saying, "You intended to harm me, but God intended it for good to accomplish what is now being done, the saving of many lives" (Genesis 50:20). Jacob and all his descendants then move to Egypt and settle in the land of Goshen.

There is a 400-year gap between the end of the book of Genesis and the first chapter of Exodus. During this time, the Israelites grow into a large community. The pharaohs who come to power forget what Joseph has done for their forefathers. The Egyptians then enslave the Israelites and commit other atrocities against them, ultimately planning to eliminate the Israelites as a distinct people (Exodus 1:8–22).

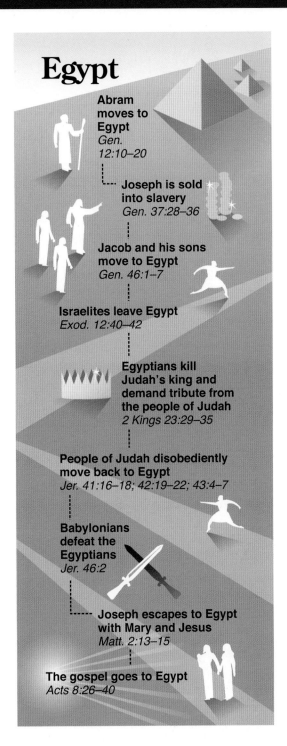

Egypt

Abram moves to Egypt
Gen. 12:10–20

Joseph is sold into slavery
Gen. 37:28–36

Jacob and his sons move to Egypt
Gen. 46:1–7

Israelites leave Egypt
Exod. 12:40–42

Egyptians kill Judah's king and demand tribute from the people of Judah
2 Kings 23:29–35

People of Judah disobediently move back to Egypt
Jer. 41:16–18; 42:19–22; 43:4–7

Babylonians defeat the Egyptians
Jer. 46:2

Joseph escapes to Egypt with Mary and Jesus
Matt. 2:13–15

The gospel goes to Egypt
Acts 8:26–40

In their distress, the Israelites cry out to God. He hears their cries and raises up Moses to deliver the Israelites from Egyptian captivity. Moses is born during the time of the Egyptian decree that all male Hebrew babies are to be killed. Moses' mother hides him in a basket on the Nile River, where Pharaoh's daughter finds and adopts him, raising him in Pharaoh's palace (Exodus 2:1–10).

Years later, after murdering an Egyptian for abusing an Israelite, Moses flees the country (Exodus 2:11–15). For years, Moses tends sheep in the desert, until one day he encounters God in the form of a "burning bush." God speaks to Moses, telling him that he has seen the misery of his people and he intends to do something about it. God commands, "So now, go. I am sending you to Pharaoh to bring my people the Israelites out of Egypt" (Exodus 3:10).

So, 40 years later, Moses returns to Egypt to lead his people out of Egypt. When Pharaoh is reluctant to let God's people leave Egypt, God sends a series of ten plagues on Egypt until Pharaoh finally releases them (Exodus 5–12). Pharaoh then changes his mind, deciding to pursue the Israelites. However, God saves the Israelites by parting the Red Sea and destroying the Egyptian army (Exodus 14).

Even after the Israelites' exodus, Egypt continues to play an important role in the biblical story. The Israelites complain about their living conditions in their 40-year travels to the Promised Land, often suggesting it would be better to return to Egypt (Exodus 14:11–12; 16:3; Numbers 14:3; 21:5). Several times, God also warns his people not to "go" to Egypt (Jeremiah 42:19; Isaiah 31:1).

Once the Israelites possess the Promised Land, Israel shares a border with Egypt. During their history, they fight three wars with Egypt. Israel also displeases God by seeking alliances with Egypt rather than trusting him to protect them (Isaiah 31:1). God repeatedly reminds his people of his trustworthiness by referring to himself as "the God who brought you out of Egypt" (Deuteronomy 5:6; Judges 2:1; 1 Samuel 10:18).

In New Testament times, Egypt is part of the Roman Empire. Jesus' parents take him to live there after they are warned by an angel to flee their hometown of Bethlehem. This fulfills a prophecy given by Hosea about the Messiah (Matthew 2:13–15; Hosea 11:1).

On the day of Pentecost, visitors from Egypt are among those in the crowd when the Holy Spirit comes upon the disciples in Jerusalem and they speak in languages they have never learned. Later, Stephen and Paul reference God bringing his people out of Egypt in their sermons explaining the Christian faith (Acts 7; 13:16–20).

When spoken of prophetically, Egypt often stands for evil or for bondage and slavery. The final mention of Egypt in the Bible is found in the book of Revelation. John speaks about two witnesses who will prophesy for three and a half years before they are killed in the city in which Jesus was crucified—Jerusalem—saying that the city is "figuratively called Sodom and Egypt" (Revelation 11:8).

MESOPOTAMIA

Mesopotamia, meaning "land between the rivers," is the Greek name for the fertile region between the Tigris and Euphrates Rivers. The majority of the region is found in modern-day Iraq, Kuwait, and Syria.

The garden of Eden is in Mesopotamia, situated between two of the four rivers that watered the garden, the Tigris and Euphrates (Genesis 2:14). Following the fall of humankind, Adam and Eve are driven out of the garden of Eden, making its exact location a mystery (Genesis 3).

The story of the tower of Babel takes place in Babylonia. At this point, humans are still speaking one common language. In their arrogance, they desire to make a name for themselves, so they decide to build a tower that reaches the sky. As a result, God confuses their languages and scatters them throughout the region, giving rise to the nations of the ancient world (Genesis 11:1 – 9).

It is in Mesopotamia that Abraham, the "father of many nations" (Genesis 17:4), first hears God calling him to leave his homeland (Genesis 12:1). God promises to bless the peoples of the earth through his descendants (Acts 7:2 – 4; Genesis 12:2 – 3). When the time comes for Abraham's son Isaac to marry, Abraham sends his servant to his homeland in Mesopotamia to find Isaac a wife. The servant returns with Rebekah (Genesis 24). Rebekah later sends her son Jacob to her homeland, where he marries and has children (Genesis 27:46 – 30:24). God renames Jacob, Israel, and through his bloodline comes the nation of Israel (Genesis 32:28).

Years later, during the time of the judges, the nation of Israel turns from following God. Enemies from Mesopotamia defeat Israel until God raises up Othniel to deliver them (Judges 3:7 – 11).

During the time of the kingdoms of Israel and Judah, the Assyrian and Babylonian empires come to power in Mesopotamia. The Assyrian Empire conquers the northern kingdom of Israel and relocates its people (2 Kings 17:6). The Babylonian Empire in turn conquers Assyria and the southern kingdom of Judah. Many Israelites are carried into exile in Babylon, in the southwestern region of Mesopotamia. The books of Daniel, Ezekiel, and Esther are written in exile. Years later when the Israelites are free to return to their homeland, many remain in Babylon and other parts of Mesopotamia.

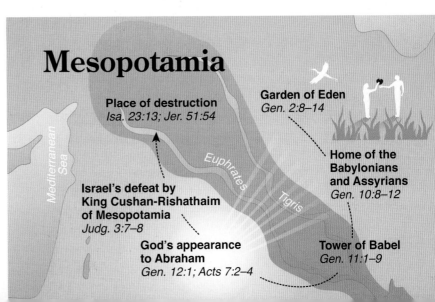

Mesopotamia

Place of destruction
Isa. 23:13; Jer. 51:54

Garden of Eden
Gen. 2:8–14

Home of the Babylonians and Assyrians
Gen. 10:8–12

Israel's defeat by King Cushan-Rishathaim of Mesopotamia
Judg. 3:7–8

God's appearance to Abraham
Gen. 12:1; Acts 7:2–4

Tower of Babel
Gen. 11:1–9

Mediterranean Sea

Euphrates

Tigris

SINAI

The Sinai Peninsula is a triangular peninsula located in the eastern portion of modern Egypt and is adjacent to modern Israel. It is bordered on the west by the Gulf of Suez and on the east by the Gulf of Aqaba, with the Red Sea to its south and the Mediterranean Sea to its north. The northern portion of the Sinai Peninsula forms a land bridge between Africa and Asia. Mount Sinai is located in the southern portion of the peninsula, about 160 miles north of the Red Sea.

The Sinai Peninsula and Mount Sinai, also called Mount Horeb, play a role in some of the most significant moments leading up to the birth of the nation of Israel. The Sinai region is the setting for a substantive portion of the Bible's Pentateuch, namely, the last 22 chapters of the book of Exodus, the entire book of Leviticus, and the first 11 chapters of the book of Numbers.

Joseph likely traverses the land bridge in the northern Sinai when he is taken to Egypt after his brothers sell him to the Midianites (Genesis 37). Later, his brothers and eventually his father cross northern Sinai on their way to buy food (Genesis 42; 43; 46).

Four hundred years later, the Sinai Peninsula takes on greater significance within the biblical narrative when it serves as a refuge for the Egyptian prince turned fugitive: Moses. He lives and tends sheep there while the Israelites are enslaved in Egypt. God speaks to Moses from a burning bush on Mount Sinai (Exodus 3:1–4), telling him that he is to lead the people of God out of Egypt.

The story of this exodus ends in dramatic fashion. God parts the Red Sea to allow Moses and his people, who had been enslaved in Egypt, to cross over to Sinai's southern shores (Exodus 14:21–22). The Israelites, standing now safely on the shore of the Red Sea, watch as Moses stretches out his hand and the waters of the Red Sea collapse back on the Egyptians who have been pursuing them all night in their chariots. The corpses of their former captors remain on the shore (Exodus 14:26–31). The Israelites then hear Moses and Miriam sing, praising God for miraculously defeating the Egyptians (Exodus 15).

The most significant event to take place during the Israelites' time in the Sinai Peninsula happens at Mount Sinai, when Moses climbs Mount Sinai and God descends on the mountain in a dark cloud to speak with him. The other Israelites hear God's voice but are not allowed to approach the mountain (Exodus 19:12). It is here that God gives Moses the Ten Commandments (Exodus 20:1–21).

The Israelites camp for a year in the Sinai Desert, also called the Desert of Sin, in the shadow of Mount Sinai. They witness the Lord leading them in a pillar of cloud by day and a pillar of fire by night. During this time, they construct the tabernacle with all of its furnishings and the ark of the covenant (Exodus 35:30–38:31). They witness the glory of the Lord filling the tabernacle in the form of a cloud, and they follow the cloud whenever it lifts from the tabernacle and moves (Exodus 40:34–38).

The Israelites are in the Sinai Peninsula when they receive the law with its system of sacrifices. Under Moses' direction, they make a covenant with God (Exodus 31:18; 34:1–28). Here, they first celebrate Passover and other feasts described in the law (Numbers 9:1–5).

While in Sinai, the Israelites often grumble and rebel against Moses. At one point, while Moses is still on the mountain with God, the Israelites demand that Moses' brother, Aaron, construct other gods for them. Shockingly, Aaron obliges and creates a golden calf, which the Israelites then begin to worship (Exodus 32). The people complain that they have nothing to eat, and God faithfully supplies them with manna (a food that miraculously appeared on the ground each day) and quail (Exodus 16:1–36). During this season, God often refers to the Israelites as "stiff-necked."

God then instructs Moses to take a census of all of the Israelites except the tribe of Levi (Numbers 1:49) while preparing to enter the Promised Land. Moses counts over 603,550 men of fighting age (Numbers 1:1–46).

After the Israelites have been in the Desert of Sinai for two years, two months, and 20 days, the cloud lifts from the tabernacle. The pillar of cloud directs the Israelites to move into the Desert of Paran, in the northeastern corner of the Sinai Peninsula, a short distance from the Promised Land (Numbers 10:11–16).

The Israelites are encamped in the Desert of Paran when Moses sends twelve spies to explore Canaan, the Promised Land. Those present hear the frightful report of ten of the spies, claiming that the land is good and fruitful but inhabited by giants. They also hear two spies, Joshua and Caleb, encourage them to go up and take the land which God has given them, declaring that God is able to give them victory.

The Israelites choose to believe the fearful spies, deciding not to enter the land. As a result, that generation is forbidden from entering the Promised Land and spends 40 years wandering in the Sinai wilderness until all but Joshua and Caleb have passed away.

Sinai

God speaks to Moses from a burning bush
Exod. 3:1–4

The Lord descends on the mountain and speaks with Moses
Exod. 19:18–23

A covenant is made between God and the Israelites
Exod. 31:18; 34:1–28

A census is taken of the tribes of Israel
Num. 1:1–19

Israelites celebrate Passover
Num. 9:1–5

Mediterranean Sea JERUSALEM
Dead Sea
EGYPT
SINAI PENINSULA
ARABIA
Red Sea

FIRST-CENTURY ISRAEL

Throughout his life, Jesus travels to many of the cities in Judea and the surrounding regions. We know very little about some of these cities, such as Bethany and Bethsaida, other than what the biblical narratives tell us. However, other cities, such as Jerusalem and Jericho, are the subject of continual archaeological study.

Bethlehem of Judea, meaning "House of Bread," is the birthplace of Jesus, "the bread of life" (John 6:35). His birth in this small town—and ancestral home to the house of David—foreshadows his later ministry to "the least, the last, and the lost," or those on the margins of society.

Jesus is raised in Nazareth, a small village in Galilee of no importance to either the Roman or Jewish authorities. As a result, many reject Jesus as a prophet, one disciple stating before meeting Jesus: "Nazareth! Can anything good come from there?" (John 1:44–46).

Jesus' first miracle of turning water into wine occurs at a wedding feast in Cana. Soon after, he begins his ministry preaching in Capernaum, a small fishing village near the Sea of Galilee (Matthew 4:12–17). It is from this village that he calls the first apostles to "fish for people" (Matthew 4:19; Mark 3:13–19).

Peter, one of Jesus' disciples, first proclaims Jesus is the "Messiah, the Son of the living God" in the Roman city of Caesarea Philippi (Matthew 16:13–19).

While traveling through Sychar, a major city in Samaria, Jesus encounters a woman at a well and reveals his identity as the Messiah (John 4:4–42). At this time, the Samaritan people are exiles who were deposited in Israel's land by the Assyrians, causing tension between the Jews and Samaritans. Jesus' interaction with a Samaritan and a woman would have been controversial. His inclusion of these despised peoples displays God's greater plan of salvation beyond the Jews.

Jericho, believed to be the oldest continually inhabited city on earth, is located near the Jordan River. Known as "the city of palm trees and springs," Jericho is an attractive city to Roman conquerors. In the Old Testament, the account of the battle of Jericho describes Israel's army conquering the city by faith (Joshua 5:13–6:25). Later in history, when Jesus passes through Jericho, he heals two blind men (Matthew 20:29–34). Later, Jesus feasts with Zacchaeus, a despised tax collector, after Zacchaeus publicly repents (Luke 19:1–10).

Jerusalem, known as the City of the Great King, is referenced in Scripture more than any other location. During Jesus' life, it is the most significant city in the province of Judea as well as the epicenter of the Jewish faith and the temple. Jesus spends a great amount of time in Jerusalem proclaiming God's kingdom through preaching, signs, and wonders. While the earthly Jerusalem is the place of Jesus' crucifixion, the New Jerusalem is described as a bride adorned for her husband in God's coming kingdom (Revelation 21:2).

First-Century Israel: The Land of Jesus

SYRIA

CAESAREA PHILIPPI
Declared by Peter to be the Messiah
Matt. 16:13–19

CAPERNAUM
First starts to preach
Matt. 4:12–17

Chooses Matthew as a disciple
Matt. 9:9–13

Heals a Roman officer's slave
Luke 7:1–10

Selects the 12 apostles
Mark 3:13–19

CANA
Changes water into wine
John 2:1–11

GALILEE

Sea of Galilee

BETHSAIDA
Heals a blind man
Mark 8:22–26

GERASENES
Cures a demon-possessed man
Luke 8:26–39

JORDAN RIVER
Baptized by John
Matt. 3:13–17

DECAPOLIS
Heals a deaf man with a speech defect
Mark 7:31–35

Feeds four thousand people
Mark 8:1–9

NAZARETH
Grows up
Matt. 2:21–23

Works as a carpenter
Mark 6:1–3a

Rejected by people in his hometown
Mark 6:1–6

NAIN
Raises a widow's son from the dead
Luke 7:11–15

SAMARIA

SYCHAR
Meets a Samaritan woman at a well
John 4:4–42

Jordan River

PEREA

PEREA
Blesses little children
Mark 10:13–16

Speaks to a rich man about eternal life
Matt. 19:16–24

GETHSEMANE
Betrayed and arrested
John 18:1–14

JERUSALEM
Astounds the teachers in the temple
Luke 2:41–50

Drives the money changers from the temple
John 2:13–17

Meets Nicodemus at night
John 3:1–13

Heals a man on the Sabbath
John 5:1–15

Forgives an adulterous woman
John 8:1–11

Shares the Last Supper with his disciples
Matt. 26:26–29

Faces his trial
Luke 22:63–71

Dies by crucifixion
Luke 23:26–56

Rises from death to life
Luke 24:1–12

JUDEA

BETHANY
Raises Lazarus from the dead
John 11

Anointed by Mary
John 12:1–8

Dead Sea

BETHANY
(on the east of the Jordan)
Calls the first disciples
John 1:35–50

JERICHO
Heals blind men
Matt. 20:29–34

Meets and saves Zacchaeus, a tax collector
Luke 19:1–10

BETHLEHEM
Born
Luke 2:1–7

CITIES OF THE CHURCH

Within one generation after Jesus' death and resurrection, the early church develops from a small sect in Judaism into a widespread movement. This movement encompasses both Jews and Gentiles, or non-Jews, throughout the Roman Empire.

Jerusalem, the cultural and religious center of the Jewish people, becomes the epicenter of the early church. Before ascending to heaven, Jesus tells his followers to wait in Jerusalem until they are baptized with the Holy Spirit (Acts 1:4–5). On the day known as "the day of Pentecost" the Spirit of God descends, and over 3,000 people profess that Jesus is Lord. Throughout the following years, Jerusalem serves as an important place of counsel and commissioning (Acts 15). After the stoning of Stephen, the first

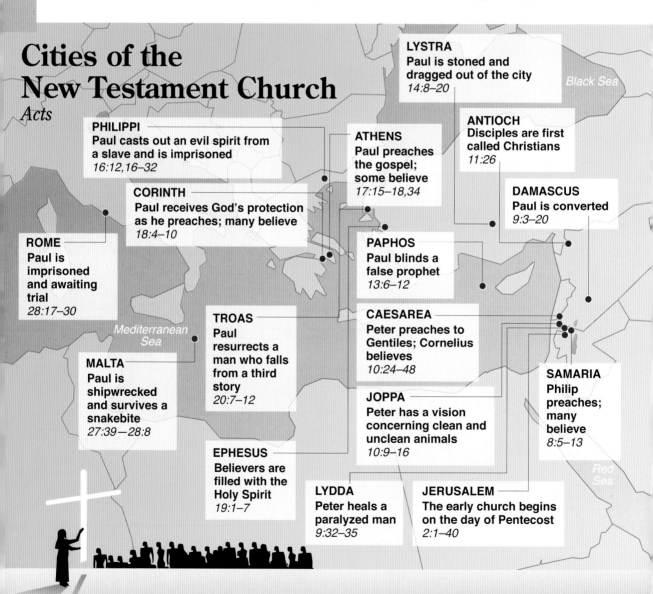

Cities of the New Testament Church

Acts

LYSTRA
Paul is stoned and dragged out of the city
14:8–20

Black Sea

PHILIPPI
Paul casts out an evil spirit from a slave and is imprisoned
16:12,16–32

ATHENS
Paul preaches the gospel; some believe
17:15–18,34

ANTIOCH
Disciples are first called Christians
11:26

CORINTH
Paul receives God's protection as he preaches; many believe
18:4–10

DAMASCUS
Paul is converted
9:3–20

ROME
Paul is imprisoned and awaiting trial
28:17–30

PAPHOS
Paul blinds a false prophet
13:6–12

TROAS
Paul resurrects a man who falls from a third story
20:7–12

CAESAREA
Peter preaches to Gentiles; Cornelius believes
10:24–48

Mediterranean Sea

MALTA
Paul is shipwrecked and survives a snakebite
27:39–28:8

JOPPA
Peter has a vision concerning clean and unclean animals
10:9–16

SAMARIA
Philip preaches; many believe
8:5–13

EPHESUS
Believers are filled with the Holy Spirit
19:1–7

Red Sea

LYDDA
Peter heals a paralyzed man
9:32–35

JERUSALEM
The early church begins on the day of Pentecost
2:1–40

Christian martyr, many believers leave Jerusalem, carrying the message of Jesus to other cities throughout the world.

Samaria was typically avoided by the Israelites in the first century due to past conflicts and tensions between the Samaritans and the Jews. However, one of the early church deacons, Philip, travels there proclaiming Jesus as the Messiah and healing and releasing people from evil spirits. As a result, many Samaritans become followers of Jesus (Acts 8:5–13).

While in the city of Joppa, a port city in ancient Israel, Peter is given a vision from God calling him to share the good news of Jesus beyond the people of Israel. The following day he travels to Caesarea, the spectacular capital of the Roman province of Judea, and preaches to a group of Gentiles. This moment signifies the God-directed expansion of the gospel message to include the Gentiles (Acts 10:9–48).

Antioch, a chief city in the Roman Empire with a large Jewish population (Acts 11:19–30), is where the term "Christian" is first applied to the disciples of Jesus (Acts 11:26). After hearing of the many new believers in Antioch, Barnabas journeys there to witness what God is doing. He brings the apostle Paul to Antioch, and over the next year, they lead the growing church, teaching large numbers of people.

From Antioch, Paul and Barnabas embark on a journey to carry the gospel throughout the remainder of the Roman Empire. On this journey, they visit Paphos on the island of Cyprus. In Paphos they lead many to faith, including a Roman governor (Acts 13:4–12).

In Lystra, a city in what is modern-day Turkey, the citizens attempt to worship Paul and Barnabas. The Lycaonians are convinced that these men are the gods Zeus and Hermes because of the miracles they perform. Ultimately, the people stone him and leave him for dead (Acts 14:8–20). Later, on his second missionary journey, Paul returns to Lystra with Silas (Acts 16:1–5).

Greece also contains important cities in the early church. In Philippi, Paul is imprisoned for casting a demon out of a slave girl (Acts 16:12–32). During his stay in Athens, the capital of Greece, Paul reasons with Stoic and Greek philosophers in the Areopagus, or the Athenian courts. He explains that a statue to the "unknown god" describes Jesus, the Messiah: "The God who made the world ... does not live in temples built by human hands" (Acts 17:16–34).

Other notable locations in the early church include Corinth and Rome. When the apostle Paul travels to Corinth, he has a dream encouraging him to be bold. He spends over a year preaching the gospel and building the church in Corinth (Acts 18:1, 4–10). Finally, the early church flourishes in Rome, despite increasing hostility toward believers. Paul, perhaps the most important leader in the early church, spends the last years of his life imprisoned in Rome, writing letters to the churches he helped establish.

BIBLE PLACES

HEAVEN

Explaining heaven is not entirely possible, as we only "see in a mirror dimly" (1 Corinthians 13:12 RSV) on this side of eternity. However, the Bible—God's inspired and authoritative word—does provide glimpses into the heaven that awaits those who believe in him and endure to the end.

In Revelation, the last book of the Bible, God shows the apostle John "a new heaven and a new earth" (Revelation 21:1), what the prophet Isaiah had prophesied thousands of years earlier: "See, I [the Lord] will create new heavens and a new earth. The former things will not be remembered, nor will they come to mind" (Isaiah 65:17). In heaven, there is absolutely no sickness, pain, or death. Cancer and Alzheimer's are gone. Sadness and grief are gone as God wipes away all of our tears (Revelation 21:4).

The Bible explains that God and the Lamb are seated on a throne at the center of the New Jerusalem, heaven's capital city. An emerald rainbow encircles God's throne as it sits on a "sea of glass" (Revelation 4:2–6). Thunder and lightning flash from God's throne of grace and justice. Around it gather "persons from every tribe" (Revelation 5:9) as well as four supernatural beings. They sing night and day, "Holy, holy, holy is the Lord God Almighty,' who was, and is, and is to come" (Revelation 4:8).

In heaven, the "curse of Adam"—that humans sin and must die—is reversed, for "the second Adam" (Romans 5:11–14),

Jesus, has come. "No longer will there be any curse. The throne of God and of the Lamb will be in the city, and his servants will serve him" (Revelation 22:3). Finally, the effects of the fall of humankind will be felt no more. In heaven, we will be fully reconciled to God as the pure and blameless bride of Christ (Revelation 19:6–9).

While we may wonder what the new heaven and the new earth will look and feel like, these concerns will become unimportant as we find ourselves captivated by the presence of God: "Look! God's dwelling place is now among the people, and he will dwell with them. They will be his people, and God himself will be with them and be their God" (Revelation 21:3).

The new heaven and the new earth are a place of unspeakable joy. There, believers will share in "the master's happiness" (Matthew 25:21), experiencing the fullness of all that God's presence brings. We will "taste and see that the LORD is good" (Psalm 34:8). The "fruit of the Spirit" will abound in a new world filled with "love, joy, peace, forbearance, kindness, goodness, faithfulness, gentleness and self-control" (Galatians 5:22–23). When we find ourselves in the presence of the Author of life, our Creator and the Lover of our souls, we will exclaim as David does: "You make known to me the path of life; you will fill me with joy in your presence, with eternal pleasures at your right hand" (Psalm 16:11).

What the Bible Says About Heaven

A rainbow encircles the throne
Ezek. 1:26–28; Rev. 4:3

The Lord's heavenly throne
Psalm 11:4

Myriad of angels
Rev. 5:11–13

Sea of glass glowing with fire
Rev. 15:2–3

Golden altar in front of the throne
Rev. 8:3

Heavenly door
Rev. 4:1

Tribulation elders in white robes
Rev. 7:13–17

24 elders on 24 thrones dressed in white with crowns of gold on their heads
Rev. 4:4

Winged living creatures covered in eyes
Rev. 4:6–11

The souls of the martyrs under the altar
Rev. 6:9

Seven sealed scrolls
Rev. 5:1–5

Seraphim worshiping God
Isa. 6:1–3

Seven spirits before the throne
Rev. 1:4

HELL

Satan's lie to Eve in the garden of Eden is not as simple as it seems.

When Satan tells Eve, "You will not certainly die" (Genesis 3:4), he twists the word of God in a very deceptive way. Does Eve physically die with a portion of the fruit still in her mouth or stomach? No, but she does *die* in a far more profound sense: she, and all of humanity by extension, dies spiritually because of sin.

God is life itself (John 5:26). The concept of life is far greater than we can fathom. Looking at life simply as the presence of heartbeats and brainwaves is shortsighted, and, not surprisingly, this is the angle that Satan, the father of lies (John 8:44), uses to deceive Eve. "You will not certainly die," Satan says. While Eve's heart continues to beat, the moment she eats the fruit she is torn from the fellowship of God: the source of life.

John 1:4 tells us that "in [Jesus] was life, and that life was the light of all mankind." Consider the following words of Jesus:

"I am the way and the truth and the life. No one comes to the Father except through me" (John 14:6).

"Now this is eternal life: that they know you, the only true God, and Jesus Christ, whom you have sent" (John 17:3).

"Jesus said to her, 'I am the resurrection and the life. The one who believes in me will live, even though they die'" (John 11:25).

"I am the light of the world. Whoever follows me will never walk in darkness, but will have the light of life" (John 8:12).

What is life? The deep, abiding presence of God that those who follow Jesus "know in part" now and will one day know fully (1 Corinthians 13:12). This is the experience Adam and Eve knew as they walked with God in the garden before the fall (Genesis 3:8).

So, what then is hell? Hell is spiritual death. It is the eternal, conscious horror of being separated from the Source of life. Second Thessalonians 1:9 says, "[Those not in Christ] will be punished with everlasting destruction and shut out from the presence of the Lord and from the glory of his might."

Though hell is a highly unpopular subject for many people, Jesus speaks more about this subject than anyone in the Bible. He uses such language as "agony," "eternal fire," and "weeping and gnashing of teeth." These words are very disturbing, and Jesus chooses them for that very reason. To be separated from God is a misery that can scarcely be comprehended. It is bad news.

Yet this is exactly why the gospel literally means *good news*, and why Jesus is called the *Savior*. His work on the cross provides a way back into spiritual life so that all who believe will escape God's wrath in hell.

What the Bible Says About Hell

Overwhelming destruction
2 Sam. 22:5–6

Absence of God's presence
2 Thess. 1:9

A bottomless pit
Rev. 9:2

Worms that don't die and eat dead bodies
Isa. 66:24

A place of torment
Luke 16:23

Lake of fire
Rev. 20:15

A place of sorrows
Matt. 13:49–50

Gates of death
Job 17:16

A place of no rest
Rev. 14:11

Fiery lake of burning sulfur
Rev. 19:20

A place of outer darkness
Matt. 22:13

Chains of darkness
2 Pet. 2:4,9

Blazing furnace
Matt. 13:41–42

An unquenchable fire
Matt. 3:12

© TheBiblePeople.com

CHAPTER 4

QUICKLOOK
BIBLE EVENTS AND STORY LINE

BIBLE TIME LINE

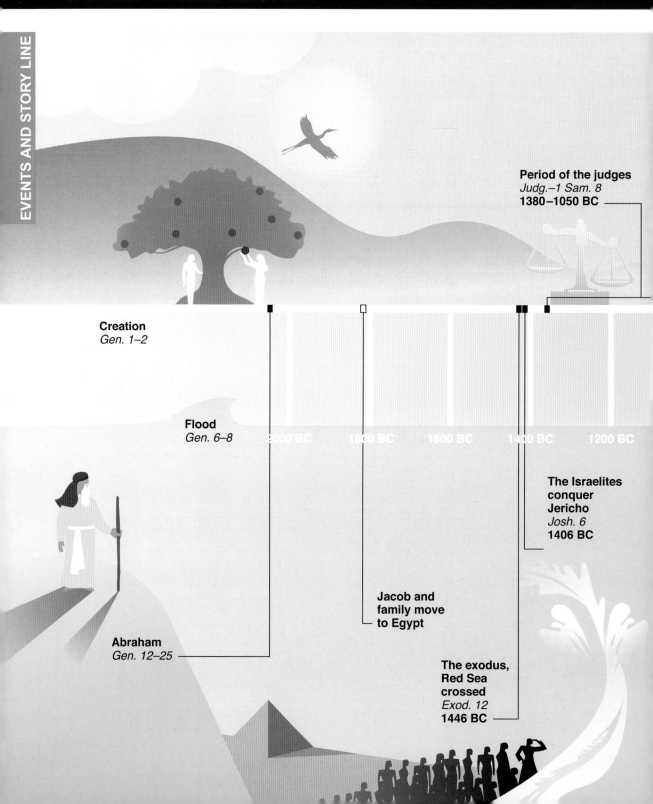

EVENTS AND STORY LINE

Period of the judges
Judg.–1 Sam. 8
1380–1050 BC

Creation
Gen. 1–2

Flood
Gen. 6–8

2000 BC   1800 BC   1600 BC   1400 BC   1200 BC

**The Israelites
conquer
Jericho**
Josh. 6
1406 BC

**Jacob and
family move
to Egypt**

Abraham
Gen. 12–25

**The exodus,
Red Sea
crossed**
Exod. 12
1446 BC

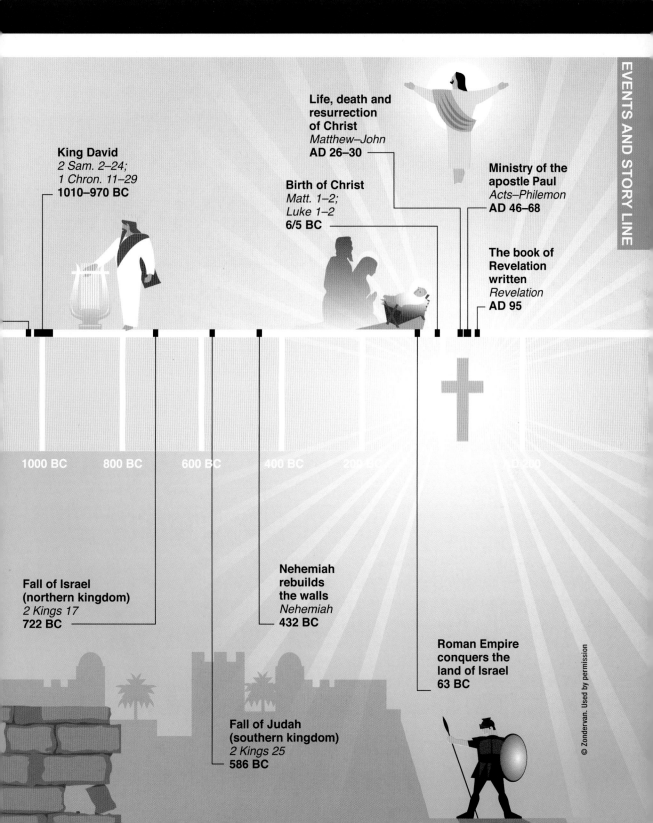

Life, death and
resurrection
of Christ
Matthew–John
AD 26–30

King David
2 Sam. 2–24;
1 Chron. 11–29
1010–970 BC

Birth of Christ
Matt. 1–2;
Luke 1–2
6/5 BC

**Ministry of the
apostle Paul**
Acts–Philemon
AD 46–68

**The book of
Revelation
written**
Revelation
AD 95

1000 BC   800 BC   600 BC   400 BC   200 BC   AD 200

**Fall of Israel
(northern kingdom)**
2 Kings 17
722 BC

**Nehemiah
rebuilds
the walls**
Nehemiah
432 BC

**Roman Empire
conquers the
land of Israel**
63 BC

**Fall of Judah
(southern kingdom)**
2 Kings 25
586 BC

BIBLE TIME LINE (CONTINUED)

One of the complexities of the Bible is that the 66 books are not assembled in chronological order. Therefore, creating a time line of historical events can bring understanding to the arc and message of Scripture.

In Genesis, God speaks the cosmos into existence. In the Garden of Eden, Adam and Eve, the first human beings, disobey God by eating fruit from the tree of knowledge of good and evil. As a result, they are cast out of the garden, severing their relationship with God, each other, and creation.

Later, God promises Abraham, Isaac, and Jacob that he will build a nation from their descendants. From their lineage come the Israelites, who eventually conquer Canaan, the Promised Land, after God rescues them from slavery in Egypt.

Once in the Promised Land, the Israelites are governed by a series of judges and kings. Eventually, civil war divides the land into two kingdoms: the northern kingdom of Israel and the southern kingdom of Judah. Because of their disobedience, the people of both nations experience God's judgment and are eventually conquered by Assyria and then Babylon, bringing an end to both nations.

Finally, Jesus ministers on earth during the time of the Roman Empire. The New Testament records details of three years of his ministry and approximately the first one hundred years of early church history.

CREATION

By the power of his Word, God speaks the world into existence. The Bible opens with these words: "In the beginning God created the heavens and the earth. Now the earth was formless and empty, darkness was over the surface of the deep, and the Spirit of God was hovering over the waters" (Genesis 1:1–2). The story of creation displays God's majestic authority and wisdom.

The six days of creation follow a parallel pattern, repeating the words, "and God said," followed by an activity of creation. In days one through three, God creates various environments, while on days four through six, God creates the objects and creatures that will inhabit those environments. For example, on day one, God creates light; while on day four, he creates the sun, moon, and stars to continually provide light for the earth. On day two, God creates the water and the sky; on day five, he creates fish and birds to populate the water and sky. On day three, God creates plant life; on day six, he creates land animals and humans. At the end of the six days of creation, the Bible records that "God saw all that he had made, and it was very good" (Genesis 1:31).

On day six, God creates the crown jewel of his creation: humankind. Unlike everything else in creation, male and female are made in his image (Genesis 1:26–27). God forms the first man, Adam, from the dust of the ground, then breathes "the breath of life" into his nostrils, making him a living being (Genesis 2:7). From the rib of Adam, God creates Eve, the first woman (Genesis 2:21–23). The man and woman are both naked, and they feel no shame (Genesis 2:25).

On day seven, God rests from work. He blesses and makes this day holy because on that day, he "rested from all the work of creating that he had done" (Genesis 2:3). In the creation account, God establishes a pattern of work and rest that he will later teach his people, the Israelites, to practice.

Adam and Eve dwell in this garden paradise filled with every good thing God has made (Genesis 2:8–9). God gives them stewardship, or responsibility, over the earth (Genesis 1:26–28), and he visits and walks alongside them (Genesis 3:8). God tells them that they may eat from any tree in the garden, but they are not to eat from "the tree of the knowledge of good and evil," for that will bring death (Genesis 2:16–17; 3:2–3).

Creation: Parallel Days
Genesis 1

Day 1: Light	**Day 4: Sun and moon**
Day 2: Water and sky	**Day 5: Fish and birds**
Day 3: Plant life	**Day 6: Animals and people**

Beautiful! God's power, wisdom and sense of order are revealed in the parallels between days 1–3 and 4–6.

FALL OF HUMANKIND

God creates the world "good" (Genesis 1:31). Tragically, humans choose to believe the lies of a serpent (Genesis 3:1–7) rather than trusting their Creator. As a result, sin enters the world, and the perfect harmony of creation becomes fractured.

When this "fall" from grace occurs, three primary relationships are broken:

- Humanity's relationship with God
- Humanity's relationship with others
- Humanity's relationship with the created world

After Adam and Eve rebel against God, he banishes them from the garden of Eden, where they once enjoyed a close relationship with him (Genesis 3:23–24). Because of God's holiness, he is unable to be in the presence of sin (Habakkuk 1:13). Therefore, he can no longer remain in close fellowship with humanity.

Not only is humanity's relationship with God shattered because of sin, but human relationships become fractured as well. Adam and Eve's son Cain murders his brother Abel (Genesis 4), clearly displaying how a once harmonious world is now filled with conflict and strife. The many biblical stories involving war, hatred, and sexual infidelity continue to illustrate this reality.

The fall also fractures humanity's relationship with the rest of creation. Whereas Adam and Eve once enjoyed cultivating the ground, the earth now becomes hostile toward humanity (Genesis 3:18). Plants grow thorns. Animals are killed. The same rain that sustains life now creates floods and blizzards, and the ground that supplies food now quakes (Luke 21:11) and groans in frustration (Romans 8:20).

Though sin wreaks havoc on God's creation, its consequences do not have the final word. From the moment humanity sins, God is already making provision for how he will reverse the fall (Genesis 3:15), bringing One who will usher in a new and everlasting kingdom (Daniel 2:44). God's plan of salvation reaches its culmination in Jesus, the Savior. Jesus alone is the remedy for every fracture created by the fall.

Jesus' death on the cross pays for the sins of all who put their faith in him. The work of Jesus' sacrifice on the cross creates a bridge back to a positive relationship between God and humanity (2 Corinthians 5:17–21). Jesus also restores interpersonal relationships. Being God in the flesh (John 1:14), Jesus is the supreme example of love (John 13:35), and through his example—and his Spirit—Christians are empowered to display God's love to the world (Galatians 5:22–23).

But what about the fallen world? Jesus' resurrection from death conquers the grip that sin once had on this world (John 14:30; Revelation 1:18). The world will soon be restored in its proper "good" order, and pain, suffering, and death will be no more (Revelation 21:4). Also, the hostilities of the environment will be put away as modeled by the peaceful coexistence between animals in heaven (Isaiah 11:6).

Because of God's grace, the story of the fall becomes a story of the hope of reconciliation and glory (Ephesians 1:18). From the beginning, God promises a Deliverer who will one day restore our relationship with God (2 Corinthians 5:17–21) and with others (1 John 4:7), making all things new (Revelation 21–22).

Consequences of the Fall & The Hope of Heaven

Connection with God Severed
Genesis 3:22–24

Connection with God Restored
Isaiah 59:1–2

Relationships with Others Damaged
Genesis 3:7

Relationships with Others Repaired
Isaiah 2:4; Isaiah 11:6

BROKEN **RESTORED**

A World Broken
Genesis 3:17–19

A World Restored
Revelation 21:4; Isaiah 25:8

© TheBiblePeople.com

NOAH'S FLOOD

Because of humankind's wickedness, God decides to destroy the earth with a flood.

God instructs Noah, the only righteous man (Genesis 6:9), to build an ark in order to save himself, his family, and every animal.

God tells Noah to use cypress wood to construct rooms and to include a roof with an opening beneath it, three decks, and a door on the ark's side (Genesis 6:14–16).

After Noah loads all the food, his family, and the animals onto the ark, God closes the door behind them (Genesis 7:16). Seven days later, the flood begins. Springs surge from below, and rain falls for 40 days and nights, drowning everything on earth. Then the rain stops.

It takes approximately one year for the water to recede. Once Noah is on dry land, he builds an altar and offers burnt offerings to the Lord. When the Lord smells the sacrifice, he says in his heart, "Never again will I curse the ground because of humans, even though every inclination of the human heart is evil from childhood. And never again will I destroy all living creatures, as I have done" (Genesis 8:21).

God then reminds Noah of the same words he spoke to Adam: "Be fruitful and increase in number and fill the earth" (Genesis 9:1; 1:28). God says to Noah and his sons: "I now establish my covenant with you … Never again will all life be destroyed by the waters of flood; never again will there be a flood to destroy the earth." As a sign and reminder of that promise, God sets the rainbow in the clouds (Genesis 9:8–17).

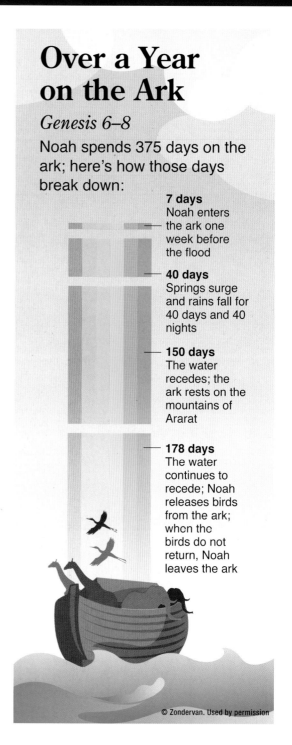

Over a Year on the Ark

Genesis 6–8

Noah spends 375 days on the ark; here's how those days break down:

7 days
Noah enters the ark one week before the flood

40 days
Springs surge and rains fall for 40 days and 40 nights

150 days
The water recedes; the ark rests on the mountains of Ararat

178 days
The water continues to recede; Noah releases birds from the ark; when the birds do not return, Noah leaves the ark

© Zondervan. Used by permission

TOWER OF BABEL

At the tower of Babel, God confuses humanity for its disobedience to his commands.

After the flood, Noah and his sons are instructed to be fruitful and multiply, to repopulate the whole earth (Genesis 9:1). They ignore this mandate and instead drift to the east of where the ark landed on Mount Ararat. They settle together on a plain in Shinar, which is probably in the region of Mesopotamia, between the Tigris and Euphrates.

There all of the people share a common language and a common goal: to make a name for themselves. They work together to build a tower to reach the heavens so they won't have to scatter over the earth—something God specifically commanded them to do (Genesis 11:4). Their actions displease the Lord.

The Lord comes down "to see the city and the tower" (Genesis 11:5). God declares that nothing will be impossible for the people if they continue to have the ability to communicate and fully understand one another (Genesis 11:5–7). God decides to halt their construction project by confusing their languages (Genesis 11:7). This event is referred to as "the tower of Babel" because the word "babel" sounds similar to the Hebrew word for "confused."

The people then aban-don the tower project, finally scattering over the whole earth (Genesis 11:8). The sons of Ham move southwest, settling in the region of Africa. The sons of Japheth migrate northwest, settling the region of modern-day Europe, while the sons of Shem move northeast, settling in Asia, or the modern-day Near and Middle East.

All three sons are fruitful and multiply, repopulating the earth. The biblical narrative then follows the descendants of Shem. Ten generations later, Abraham, "the father of many nations" and the forefather of Jesus, is born in Shem's line.

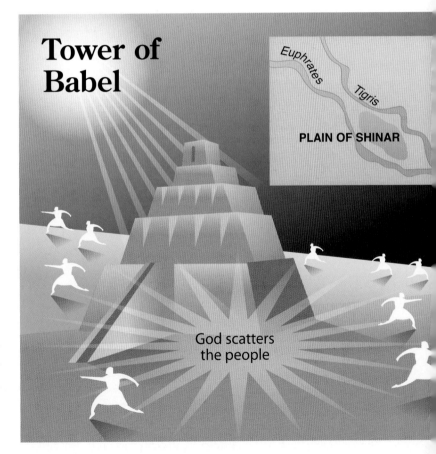

Tower of Babel

Euphrates

Tigris

PLAIN OF SHINAR

God scatters the people

CALL OF ABRAHAM

When Abraham is 75 years old, God instructs him to leave his home to follow him, promising: "I will make you into a great nation, and I will bless you ... all peoples on earth will be blessed through you" (Genesis 12:1–3).

Abraham doesn't know where he is going, but he obeys in faith and goes wherever God leads (Hebrews 11:8–9).

Although Abraham and his wife, Sarah, are childless, God promises them that they will have more children than the stars in the sky (Genesis 15:5).

Years later, and after moments of doubt, God fulfills this promise with the birth of a son, Isaac. From Abraham's lineage come the nation of Israel and eventually the Savior, Jesus.

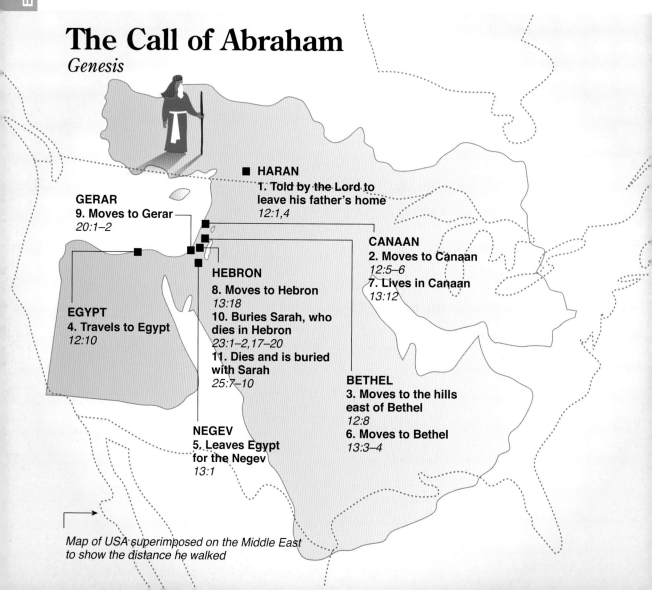

The Call of Abraham
Genesis

HARAN
1. Told by the Lord to leave his father's home
12:1,4

GERAR
9. Moves to Gerar
20:1–2

CANAAN
2. Moves to Canaan
12:5–6
7. Lives in Canaan
13:12

HEBRON
8. Moves to Hebron
13:18
10. Buries Sarah, who dies in Hebron
23:1–2, 17–20
11. Dies and is buried with Sarah
25:7–10

EGYPT
4. Travels to Egypt
12:10

BETHEL
3. Moves to the hills east of Bethel
12:8
6. Moves to Bethel
13:3–4

NEGEV
5. Leaves Egypt for the Negev
13:1

Map of USA superimposed on the Middle East to show the distance he walked

PROMISES MADE

Abraham receives and believes a very significant promise from God. This great promise has three parts.

First, God promises to make Abraham "the father of many nations" (Genesis 17:4). God promises this when Abraham and his wife are old and have no children. Second, God promises to be Abraham's God and the God of the descendants after him.

Third, God promises to give Abraham and his descendants the land of Canaan, known as the Promised Land (Genesis 17:4–8).

The apostle Paul uses Abraham's life as proof that righteousness comes through faith rather than works: "Abraham 'believed God, and it was credited to him as righteousness'" (Galatians 3:6).

Promises Made to Abraham
Genesis

His name will be made great; he will be a blessing
12:2b,3c

Those who bless him will be blessed
12:3a

Those who curse him will be cursed
12:3b

He will become a great nation and be blessed
12:2a

His descendants will be given Canaan
12:6–7; 17:8

He will have many descendants
13:14–17

His own son will be his heir
15:2–5

Sarah will give birth to a son
18:8–11

He will be the father of many nations
17:1–8

Through his offspring all nations will be blessed
22:15–18

BIRTH AND CALL OF MOSES

Moses is born during Israel's captivity in Egypt. When the Egyptian pharaoh orders all Hebrew baby boys killed to prevent the Israelite population from growing (Exodus 1:15–22), Moses' mother hides baby Moses in the reeds by the Nile River. He is eventually found and raised by Pharaoh's daughter (Exodus 2:5–10) in the Egyptian palace.

Eighty years later, Moses is living as a refugee on the Sinai Peninsula. He has been raising sheep (Exodus 2:21; 3:1) since he fled Egypt after murdering an Egyptian who was abusing a Hebrew slave (Exodus 2:11–15). One day, Moses sees a bush burning but not being consumed, so he examines it more closely (Exodus 3:1–4). God speaks to him out of the burning bush, telling Moses that he is calling him to return to Egypt, confront Pharaoh, and lead God's people to the Promised Land (Exodus 3:5–10).

Moses

The number of times Moses does the following:

Tells Pharaoh to free God's people
10

Fasts
3

Brings water from a rock
2

Receives the Ten Commandments
2

Shout-Outs

How many times is Moses mentioned in the Bible?

818

What percentage of the Bible did Moses write?*

15.7%
187
chapters**

* *Based on number of chapters*
**Approximately

Ages 1–40

Born after Pharaoh orders that all Hebrew baby boys be killed
Exod. 1:15—2:2a

Hidden by his Hebrew mother, who fears for his life
Exod. 2:2b–4

Adopted by Pharaoh's daughter
Exod. 2:5–10

Grows up; flees from Egypt
Exod. 2:11–15

Ages 41–80

Marries a Midianite woman
Exod. 2:16–22

Has a son
Exod. 2:22

Hears God speaking from a burning bush
Exod. 3:1–6

Chosen to lead the Israelites out of Egypt
Exod. 3:7–10

Ages 81–120

Returns to Egypt
Exod. 4:18–20

Confronts Pharaoh
Exod. 7:10–11:10

Leads the people to the promised land
Exod. 14–40

Buried
Deut. 34:1–12

PLAGUES AND THE EXODUS

After 400 years of enslavement in Egypt, God hears the cries of the Israelite people (Exodus 2:23–25). Moses, a Hebrew raised in the Egyptian court, is set apart from birth for God's special purpose (Exodus 2:1–10). God calls Moses to lead the Israelites out of Egypt to freedom in the land God promised to their forefathers (Exodus 3:16–17).

God sends Moses to Pharaoh requesting permission for the Israelites to go into the wilderness and worship their God. However, God reveals to Moses that Pharaoh will refuse, allowing God to display his power and wonders in Egypt while delivering the Israelites from oppression (Exodus 3:16–22). Upon hearing God's plan, the Israelite elders fall in worship to the Lord, grateful that he sees the misery of the Israelite people and cares for them (Exodus 4:27–31).

After the final plague, Pharaoh finally decides to release the Israelites. God gives his people favor with the Egyptians, who, in their eagerness to see the Israelites leave, freely supply them with gold, silver, and clothing (Exodus 12:35–36).

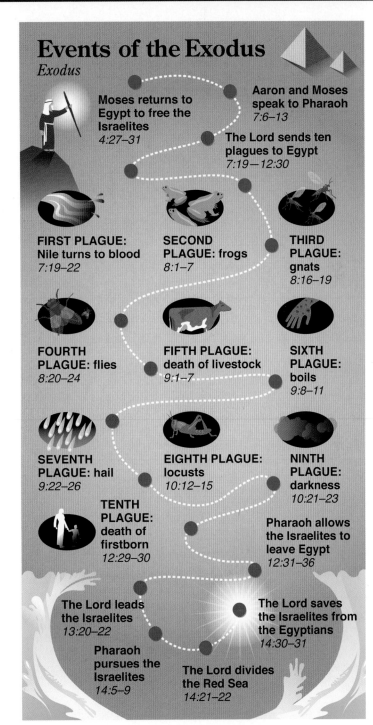

Events of the Exodus
Exodus

Moses returns to Egypt to free the Israelites
4:27–31

Aaron and Moses speak to Pharaoh
7:6–13

The Lord sends ten plagues to Egypt
7:19–12:30

FIRST PLAGUE: Nile turns to blood
7:19–22

SECOND PLAGUE: frogs
8:1–7

THIRD PLAGUE: gnats
8:16–19

FOURTH PLAGUE: flies
8:20–24

FIFTH PLAGUE: death of livestock
9:1–7

SIXTH PLAGUE: boils
9:8–11

SEVENTH PLAGUE: hail
9:22–26

EIGHTH PLAGUE: locusts
10:12–15

NINTH PLAGUE: darkness
10:21–23

TENTH PLAGUE: death of firstborn
12:29–30

Pharaoh allows the Israelites to leave Egypt
12:31–36

The Lord leads the Israelites
13:20–22

The Lord saves the Israelites from the Egyptians
14:30–31

Pharaoh pursues the Israelites
14:5–9

The Lord divides the Red Sea
14:21–22

THE GIVING OF THE LAW

In the desert, God prepares the Israelites to enter the Promised Land. He desires for his people to be witnesses to the surrounding pagan nations that the God of Israel is the one true God. As a people who follow a just and holy God, the Israelites are to be governed by his ways, not the ways of the world.

God communicates his law to Moses on Mount Sinai. Moses not only orally retells the law to the Israelites, but also records the law within the first five books of the Bible: Genesis, Exodus, Leviticus, Numbers, and Deuteronomy. These books are known together as the Pentateuch.

The lives of the Israelites, the people of God, are to be guided and shaped by the law: "These commandments that I give you today are to be on your hearts. Impress them on your children. Talk about them when you sit at home and when you walk along the road, when you lie down and when you get up. Tie them as symbols on your hands and bind them on your foreheads. Write them on the doorframes of your houses and on your gates" (Deuteronomy 6:6–9).

Within the law, there are 613 distinct commands covering subjects that address nearly every aspect of life. The law covers how and when people should worship God, when they should hold feasts and festivals, and how they should plant their crops. The law covers the relationship between masters and slaves. The law includes instructions for dealing with communicable diseases, what the Israelites can and cannot eat, what kinds of clothing they can and cannot wear, and what kinds of sexual behavior they can and cannot engage in.

The law communicates God's heart for the least, the last, and the lost (Deuteronomy 10:18; 24:17–19). The Israelites are to be markedly different from the rest of the world because they are a people set apart by God. The law reflects both God's compassion and his holiness and justice. This is evident in how the followers of God treat one another, especially the foreigner, the orphan, and the widow—the vulnerable and oppressed—among them.

In the New Testament, the law and its commandments are described as good but incapable of making people righteous, because no one is able to keep the law in its entirety (Galatians 3:21). Until the Promised One arrives, humanity needs the law because it's how we know that we sin against God, or break the law (Galatians 3:19). The law makes us aware of our sin, pointing us to Jesus, the only One who can fulfill the requirements of the law through the nature of his life and his death on the cross. Jesus takes the "written code" that stands against us and nails it to the cross, defeating the power of sin and death over us (Colossians 2:13–15).

The New Testament makes it clear that Christians are no longer subject to the law but are instead under grace (Romans 6:14; 7:1–4; 2 Corinthians 3:7–18; Galatians 3:10–13). While the law makes us aware of our sin, only faith in Jesus removes our sin from us: "For what the law was powerless to do because it was weakened by the flesh, God did by sending his own Son in the likeness of sinful flesh to be a sin offering" (Romans 8:3).

The Giving of the Law

The Pentateuch offers approximately 613 laws that span 34 subjects. Here is a list of the amount of laws that relate to each topic.

Lepers and leprosy 4   Prayer and blessings 4

Injuries and damages 4   The firstborn 4   Criminal laws 7

Prophecy 3   Signs and symbols 5   Agriculture and animal husbandry 7

Clothing 3   Treatment of the Gentiles 6   Treatment of the law 6

The king 7   Vows, oaths and swearing 7   God 10   Nazirites 10   Property and property rights 11

The poor and unfortunate 13   Business practices 14   Loving others 14   Rituals and impurity 16

Wars 16   The Sabbath and Jubilee years 17   Employees, servants and slaves 19

Marriage, divorce and family 23   Punishment and restitution 24

Tithes, taxes and gifts 24   Forbidden sexual relations 25

Dietary laws 27   High priests, priests and Levites 30

The temple, the sanctuary and sacred objects 33   Time and seasons 36

The court and judicial procedures 36

Idolatry, idolaters and idolatrous practices 46

Sacrifices and offerings 102

*Source: Adapted from http://www.hisglory.us/

FORTY YEARS IN THE WILDERNESS

The Israelites escape Egypt in miraculous fashion. God sends seven plagues, including frogs, locusts, bloody water, and more, prompting Pharaoh to release the Israelites from slavery. Then, the Israelites witness God parting the Red Sea, allowing them to pass through on dry land to escape their enemies. God faithfully directs their movements, leading them with a pillar of cloud by day and a pillar of fire by night.

Next, the Israelites travel to the Desert of Shur (Exodus 15:22). When they finally find water after three days without, the water they find is polluted, so they begin to complain. After God miraculously makes the water drinkable, Moses, their leader, tells the Israelites that they will be free of the diseases they had in Egypt if they will listen to and obey God (Exodus 15:26–27).

After Elim, where they find plenty of fresh water (Exodus 15:27), the Israelites travel to the Desert of Sin in the Sinai Peninsula (Exodus 16:1). There, they complain again, this time due to hunger. Again, God miraculously provides, sending manna, or bread from heaven (Exodus 16). Moses instructs them to gather only what they need for the day (Exodus 16:16), as God will provide each morning. Some do not trust God, so they hoard some manna for the next day. Maggots destroy the food, and Moses gets angry (Exodus 16:20).

Next, the Israelites camp at Rephidim, where God again miraculously provides water for his complaining people (Exodus 17:1–7). While the Israelites are there, the Amalekites attack them. God gives the

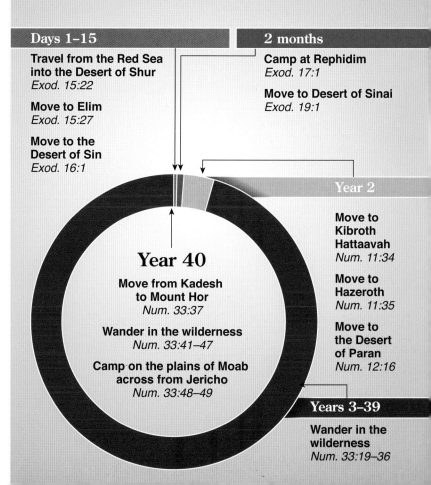

The Israelites' 40 Years in the Desert

Days 1–15

Travel from the Red Sea into the Desert of Shur
Exod. 15:22

Move to Elim
Exod. 15:27

Move to the Desert of Sin
Exod. 16:1

2 months

Camp at Rephidim
Exod. 17:1

Move to Desert of Sinai
Exod. 19:1

Year 2

Move to Kibroth Hattaavah
Num. 11:34

Move to Hazeroth
Num. 11:35

Move to the Desert of Paran
Num. 12:16

Year 40

Move from Kadesh to Mount Hor
Num. 33:37

Wander in the wilderness
Num. 33:41–47

Camp on the plains of Moab across from Jericho
Num. 33:48–49

Years 3–39

Wander in the wilderness
Num. 33:19–36

Israelites victory as long as Moses keeps his hands raised. When Moses tires, others help support his arms until the battle is over (Exodus 17:8–16). From Rephidim, the Israelites move to the Desert of Sinai, where God meets with Moses "face to face" (Numbers 12:8), giving him the law.

Throughout the Israelites' 40 years in the desert, Moses is God's chosen leader. The Bible says of him, "Now Moses was a very humble man, more humble than anyone else on the face of the earth" (Numbers 12:3). After receiving the law, Moses then communicates it to the rest of the Israelite community (Exodus 19–31), instructing them to teach it to their children and to their children's children.

However, even after hearing God's law, the Israelites rebel by making and worshiping idols. Moses prays for the people, asking God not to destroy them (Exodus 32:7–14), then leads the Israelites to consecrate themselves to God again (Exodus 32:15–35). After the people recommit themselves to following the Lord, they construct the tabernacle, a place where the Spirit of God resides and the people can meet with him. They furnish it according to the instructions God gives Moses (Exodus 35–40).

Then, the Israelites begin traveling north toward the Promised Land. Along the way, the Israelites continue to complain, and God continues to meet their needs, though the provision is sometimes accompanied with consequences for the complaining (Numbers 11–12).

Before entering the Promised Land, Moses sends 12 spies into the area. All of the spies agree that the land is good and fruitful. Two of the spies, Joshua and Caleb, tell the Israelites to take the land God has given them. The other spies report that the people in the Promised Land are giants who are too powerful to defeat (Numbers 13). The fearful Israelites listen to the discouraging report and begin to complain again. Moses prays that God will have mercy on them, not destroying them for their lack of faith. God forgives the Israelites but decrees that they will wander in the wilderness for 40 years before entering the Promised Land, until all of them except Caleb and Joshua have died.

The Israelites then spend the next 40 years wandering in the wilderness near the Promised Land. During this time, God continues to provide for them. They have manna to eat and their clothing does not wear out (Deuteronomy 8:4; 29:5), even while they continue to complain, doubting that God will take care of them (Numbers 19:2–5; 21:4–5). During this time, God brings several judgments on the people, including sending plagues (Numbers 11:33) and fiery serpents (Numbers 21:6), but he never destroys the rebellious Israelites.

In the fortieth year after leaving Egypt, the Israelites camp near Mount Hor. While there, Moses gives the people instructions for conquering Canaan, or the Promised Land (Numbers 33:50–56), and how to divide the land among their tribes once they have arrived (Numbers 34–36). In the wilderness, an entire generation of Israelites dies. Only Joshua and Caleb remain to lead God's people across the Jordan River and into the Promised Land that awaits them.

JOURNEY TO THE PROMISED LAND

When Moses dies, Joshua becomes Israel's new leader as its people prepare to enter Canaan, the Promised Land. Forty years earlier, Moses sent in 12 spies to assess the land and its inhabitants. Ten of the spies returned saying the land was filled with giants and was impossible to conquer. The other two spies, Joshua and Caleb, encouraged God's people to enter the land, but no one listened to them. Now, 40 years later, Joshua and Caleb again stand ready to lead the battered Israelites into the land God promised so long ago.

As a sign of his presence and power, God miraculously parts the waters, allowing the Israelites to pass through. After the crossing, Joshua commands one man from each tribe to bring a stone from the river in order to erect a monument west of the Jordan. This monument is to remind future generations that God brought their ancestors into the land (Joshua 4:1–9).

Once across the river, the Israelites encounter another obstacle, the walls of Jericho. Following God's instructions, Joshua leads a silent march around the walls, once around the walls each day for six days. On the seventh day, they march around the walls six times. As they finish their final lap, Joshua instructs: "Shout! for the LORD has given you the city!" (Joshua 6:16). They shout. The walls crumble to the ground, and Jericho becomes theirs.

The Israelites' conquest of Canaan occurs in three major military campaigns under Joshua's leadership. When God provides victory, the Israelites worship him.

▶ Taking the Promised Land
Joshua

The name Joshua derives from the Hebrew name meaning "Yahweh is salvation"

BY THE NUMBERS

28
The approximate number of years Joshua leads Israel

12
The amount of stones used to erect a monument to the Lord's miracle *4:1–9*

☠ 100 ☠
Joshua's age when he dies *24:29*

JOSHUA'S VICTORIES

Conquers the land in **3** major campaigns

Defeats **31** kings

MIRACULOUS EVENTS

7 Joshua leads the people around Jericho for 7 days before the walls fall *6:1–25*

The Lord throws hailstones down on the Amorites *10:6–11*

The sun stands still for **1** day *10:13*

"Choose for yourselves this day whom you will serve . . . But as for me and my household, we will serve the LORD." 24:15

When God allows defeat, he reveals the cause: sin within the camp (Joshua 7).

Taking of the Promised Land takes 28 years. Once it is accomplished, Joshua divides the land between the 12 tribes: Reuben and Gad receive the land they previously requested east of the Jordan River, while the remaining tribes decide by lot. According to Moses' original instructions, each tribe except for the Levites receives land in proportion to their population (Joshua 15 – 19). The Levites, who are tasked with assisting the priests, receive a portion of the sacrifices instead of land (Joshua 13:14, 33). In this way, God provides for all of his people as they settle into their new homeland.

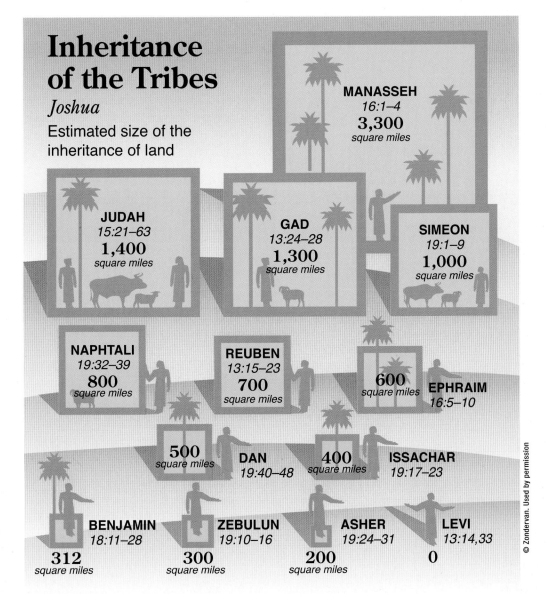

Inheritance of the Tribes

Joshua

Estimated size of the inheritance of land

MANASSEH
16:1–4
3,300
square miles

JUDAH
15:21–63
1,400
square miles

GAD
13:24–28
1,300
square miles

SIMEON
19:1–9
1,000
square miles

NAPHTALI
19:32–39
800
square miles

REUBEN
13:15–23
700
square miles

600
square miles
EPHRAIM
16:5–10

500
square miles
DAN
19:40–48

400
square miles
ISSACHAR
19:17–23

BENJAMIN
18:11–28
312
square miles

ZEBULUN
19:10–16
300
square miles

ASHER
19:24–31
200
square miles

LEVI
13:14,33
0

PERIOD OF THE JUDGES

The period of the judges of Israel spans nearly 400 years. It follows the conquest of the Promised Land and the death of Joshua. After Joshua dies, the Israelites fail to completely drive out the inhabitants of the Promised Land as the Lord commands them. During this time, the Israelites bring upon themselves a series of conquering raiders because of their disobedience. The Lord's hand is against them when they sin, causing them great distress. Then the Lord raises up judges, who save them "out of the hands of these raiders" (Judges 2:16). The period of the judges lasts until the Israelites ask the prophet Samuel, their last judge, to appoint a king to rule over them.

The book of Judges records seven distinct cycles for the nation of Israel. They move from sin to liberation and back to sin again. The Israelites sin by worshiping pagan gods, resulting in God's judgment in the form of invading nations. While under their enemies' yoke, the people repent of their sin. God then raises up a judge who liberates the people. The people continue to follow God while the judge lives but fall back into sin after the judge dies, starting the cycle again.

Othniel is Israel's first judge (Judges 3:9–10). He is the younger brother of Caleb, one of two Israelite spies whose faith and courage help lead the Israelites into the Promised Land while everyone else is afraid. Othniel, like Caleb, demonstrates courage and takes the nation of Israel to war in order to liberate it from eight years of foreign rule (Judges 3:8).

Ehud succeeds Othniel. God raises him up to deliver Israel from 18 years of Moabite rule (Judges 3:14). Ehud pretends to have a secret message for the king of Moab, assassinates him, and then leads the Israelites in battle, ultimately conquering the Moabites.

Shamgar succeeds Ehud. He personally kills over 600 enemy Philistines with an ox goad, the sharpened stick.

Israel's next judge is the prophetess Deborah. She

Cycle of the Judges

Judges

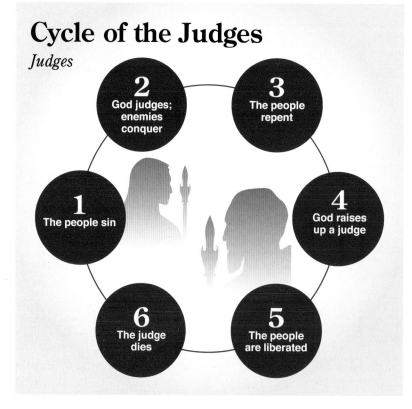

- **2** God judges; enemies conquer
- **3** The people repent
- **1** The people sin
- **4** God raises up a judge
- **6** The judge dies
- **5** The people are liberated

instructs a man named Barak to lead the Israelites against the Canaanites. Barak refuses to go unless Deborah goes with him. Deborah goes to war and prophesies that the honor for the battle will go to a woman instead of Barak. This is fulfilled when an Israelite woman kills the enemy king in his sleep (Judges 4–5).

Some time after Deborah, God raises up and transforms his next chosen judge, Gideon. An angel of the Lord approaches Gideon as he is fearfully hiding from the enemies. God calls him a "mighty warrior," a designation that Gideon later embodies as he leads the Israelites to victory over the Midianites (Judges 6–9).

Among the more notable judges to follow Gideon are Jephthah and Samson. The period of the judges of Israel ends when the people tell the prophet and judge Samuel that they want a king, in spite of God's warnings against this (1 Samuel 8:1–9).

Judges of Israel
Judges

ELON
Judges Israel for
10 years
12:11

EHUD
Leads the Israelites to strike down
10,000 Moabites
3:26–29

TOLA
Leads Israel for
23 years
10:2

JEPHTHAH
Sacrifices his daughter to fulfill his vow to the Lord
11:34–40

DEBORAH
Leads the Israelites to defeat Sisera, the commander for King Jabin
4:7,23–24

GIDEON
Has 71 sons
8:30–31

OTHNIEL
Serves as
Israel's 1st judge
3:9–10

JUDGE

IBZAN
30 sons & 30 daughters
12:9

SAMSON
Strikes down
1,000
Philistines with the fresh jawbone of a
donkey
15:15

ABDON
40
sons and
30
grandsons who ride on
70
donkeys
12:14

JAIR
30 sons
who ride on 30 donkeys
10:4

SHAMGAR
Kills 600
Philistines with a sharp
stick
3:31

DAVID'S FAMILY

David comes from Abraham's lineage, and from David's lineage eventually comes Jesus, the Messiah: "There were fourteen generations in all from Abraham to David, fourteen from David to the exile to Babylon, and fourteen from the exile to the Messiah" (Matthew 1:17).

David has at least eight wives who are named in Scripture, and an unspecified number of concubines with whom he has over 20 children. David's family experiences considerable turmoil. For example, his son Amnon rapes his half-sister, and another son, Absalom, attempts to seize David's throne.

David's first wife, Michal, the daughter of King Saul, is childless; his wife Bathsheba gives birth to Solomon, who eventually inherits the throne of Israel and is in the lineage of Jesus.

David's Family Tree

DAVID

David's wives: Michal | Abigail | Ahinoam | Maacah | Abital | Haggith | Eglah | Bathsheba | Concubine

Children of David's wives:
Kileab | Amnon | Absalom Tamar | Shephatiah | Adonijah | Ithream | Nathan Shammua Shobab SOLOMON

Naamah Rehoboam

Pharaoh's Daughter

700 Wives and 300 Concubines

DAVID: SONGWRITER

David, the shepherd boy who later becomes king of Israel, authors nearly half of the psalms (also known as songs or hymns) in Scripture. Before becoming King, David plays in the royal court, comforting King Saul (1 Samuel 16:14–23).

David writes many psalms of praise, thanksgiving, and wisdom. Psalms of praise express gratitude for God's character, while psalms of thanksgiving proclaim his great works. The psalms of wisdom celebrate God's law. David also writes imprecatory, or invoking, psalms calling for God's justice against his enemies.

David writes eight royal psalms, honoring the current kingship while pointing to the ultimate King of Israel, Jesus. David composes several of the Messianic psalms, such as Psalm 22, prophesying, or foretelling, the coming Savior.

David writes four pilgrimage psalms, a series of hymns sung by the Israelites on their ascent to Jerusalem for the Passover feast.

The majority of David's psalms are songs of lament. These songs convey human suffering while seeking refuge in God's presence. They often call on the goodness of God in the midst of suffering: "Turn to me and be gracious to me, for I am lonely and afflicted" (Psalm 25:16).

Different Types of Psalms

Imprecatory Psalms

Prayers for God's judgment against enemies
7, 35, 40, 55, 58–59, 69, 79, 109, 137, 139, 147

Royal Psalms

Psalms that extol the king of Israel (David) and point to a future, Messianic King
2, 18, 20–21, 45, 72, 101, 110, 132, 144

Wisdom Psalms
Psalms that celebrate the teaching of the Law
1, 19, 27, 37, 49, 73, 112, 119, 127–128, 133

Pilgrimage Psalms

Songs sung by ancient Israelites during their pilgrimage to Jerusalem
120–134

Praise Psalms

Psalms that offer praise to God
8, 18, 21, 29–30, 33, 36, 40–41, 66, 68, 75, 93, 103–106, 111, 113–114, 116–117, 135–136, 138, 145–150

Thanksgiving Psalms

Psalms that offer thanks to God
9, 32, 34, 65–67, 92, 105–107, 116, 118, 136, 138

Messianic Psalms

Psalms that look forward to the coming Messiah
2, 8, 16, 22, 34–35, 40–41, 45, 68–69, 89, 102, 109–110, 118

Lament Psalms

Psalms that seek God's presence during times of difficulty or crisis
3–7, 9–10, 12–14, 17, 22, 25–28, 31, 35–36, 38–44, 51–61, 64, 69–71, 74, 77, 79–80, 82–83, 85–86, 88–90, 94, 102, 108–109, 120, 123, 126, 129–130, 137, 139–143

THE UNITED KINGDOM OF ISRAEL

Until Samuel, the last in the line of Israel's judges, God's people are a loosely allied set of twelve tribes. Samuel unites the Israelites as a single nation by appointing their first king, creating a union that ultimately endures 120 years under the reign of three kings.

Samuel anoints a towering figure named Saul from the tribe of Benjamin as the first king over Israel. Though tall in stature, Saul is a humble man (1 Samuel 9:21).

God provides victory and success over the Israelites' enemies during the early years of Saul's reign (1 Samuel 11:11; 14:23). However, as Saul enjoys continued success, he becomes increasingly proud. God sends the prophet Samuel to anoint a young man named David (1 Samuel 16).

David doesn't assume the throne immediately after being anointed. He continues tending his father's sheep and serves as a musician in Saul's court. David eventually garners the attention of Israel by killing the Philistine giant, Goliath, with a shepherd's sling and a smooth stone.

Saul eventually kills himself to avoid being captured by the Philistines in battle (1 Samuel 31:1–6). Upon hearing of Saul's death, David tears his clothes and fasts in mourning. The tribe of Judah quickly recognizes David as their new king (2 Samuel 2:1–7), but those loyal to Saul wage war with David for seven years (2 Samuel 5).

David's kingship is immortalized by great victories, leading Israel in almost constant warfare. Although considered a strong leader, David's reign contains some foolish and sinful moments — namely, numbering the Israelites, which brings God's judgment on the nation (2 Samuel 24), and commit-

The Kingdom Divides

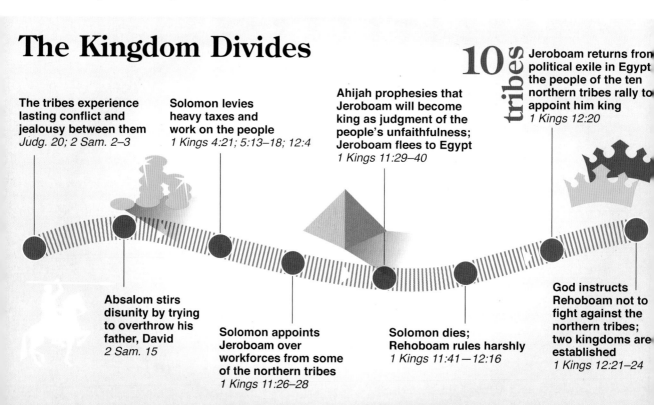

10 tribes   Jeroboam returns from political exile in Egypt; the people of the ten northern tribes rally to appoint him king
1 Kings 12:20

The tribes experience lasting conflict and jealousy between them
Judg. 20; 2 Sam. 2–3

Solomon levies heavy taxes and work on the people
1 Kings 4:21; 5:13–18; 12:4

Ahijah prophesies that Jeroboam will become king as judgment of the people's unfaithfulness; Jeroboam flees to Egypt
1 Kings 11:29–40

Absalom stirs disunity by trying to overthrow his father, David
2 Sam. 15

Solomon appoints Jeroboam over workforces from some of the northern tribes
1 Kings 11:26–28

Solomon dies; Rehoboam rules harshly
1 Kings 11:41–12:16

God instructs Rehoboam not to fight against the northern tribes; two kingdoms are established
1 Kings 12:21–24

ting adultery with Bathsheba, which results in the death of his son (2 Samuel 11–12).

David desires to build a temple for the Lord in Jerusalem, but God doesn't allow him to do so. Instead, his son Solomon builds the temple.

Once he assumes his role as king, Solomon becomes known throughout the land for his wisdom. He rules during a time of extended peace for Israel, allowing him to focus on ambitious building projects and academic pursuits. He conscripts laborers to build the Lord's temple and his own palace (1 Kings 5:13). The Levites place the ark of the covenant in the new temple, which is dedicated to the Lord. God shows his approval once again: "The temple of the LORD was filled with the cloud … the glory of the LORD filled the temple of God" (2 Chronicles 5:13–14).

Solomon's reign marks the height of Israel's splendor. However, Solomon disobeys God by taking foreign wives, who eventually lead Solomon to welcome and participate in idol worship (1 Kings 11:1–13). God ultimately pronounces judgment on Solomon, decreeing that all but one tribe of the kingdom will be torn from him when his son becomes king. This judgment ends the period of Israel as a united kingdom—dividing God's people into the northern kingdom of Israel and the southern kingdom of Judah (1 Kings 12:1–24).

United Kingdom

70,000 DEATHS Israelites die from a plague as a result of David's disobedience *2 Sam. 24:15*

40-YEAR REIGNS

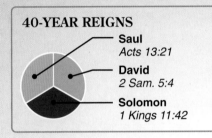

- **Saul** *Acts 13:21*
- **David** *2 Sam. 5:4*
- **Solomon** *1 Kings 11:42*

ONE SMOOTH STONE

All it took for David, the Lord's anointed, to slay the mighty Goliath *1 Sam. 17:49*

VICTORY OVER THOUSANDS
1 Sam. 18:7

David is credited with killing tens of thousands

Saul is credited with killing only thousands

WIVES & CONCUBINES

SAUL: one wife, one concubine
1 Sam. 14:50; 2 Sam. 21:8

DAVID: at least eight wives, many concubines
1 Sam. 25:44; 2 Sam. 3:2–5; 5:13; 15:16; 1 Chron. 3

SOLOMON: 700 wives, 300 concubines
1 Kings 11:3

GIFT OF WISDOM God grants King Solomon a wise and discerning heart *1 Kings 3:12*

SOLOMON'S BUILDING PROJECTS

Seven years to build the temple
1 Kings 6:38

Thirteen years to build his own palace
1 Kings 7:1

PROPHETS AND THEIR KINGS

Throughout the Old Testament, God raises up prophets to deliver his words of judgment and inspiring visions to his earthly leaders. While the prophets endure some of the harshest persecution recorded in the Bible, they remain faithful to speak God's word, regardless of the consequences. Some of their words and stories are collected in Old Testament books such as Isaiah, Micah, and Ezekiel.

Samuel is a prophet and the last judge, or leader, of the Israelites before Israel becomes a monarchy, led by an earthly king instead of God. Samuel serves during this transition period, anointing Israel's first two kings: Saul and David (in approximately 1050 and 1025 BC respectively). He prophesies and serves as an advisor to King Saul (1 Samuel 10:25). When Saul disobeys God, Samuel rebukes him sharply, telling him that the kingdom will be torn from him (1 Samuel 13:8 – 14; 15:12 – 29). Samuel then anoints David to replace Saul as king (1 Samuel 16:13).

The prophet Nathan advises King David during his reign. When David seeks Nathan's advice about building a temple for the Lord, Nathan tells him that his son will be the one to build it, not him. More importantly, Nathan says that it is through David's offspring that God will establish his everlasting kingdom: "When your days are over and you rest with your ancestors, I will raise up your offspring to succeed you, your own flesh and blood, and I will establish his kingdom" (2 Samuel 7:12). This

refers to the Messiah, Jesus, who eventually comes through David's lineage.

Later, Nathan confronts David about his affair with Bathsheba and the murder of her husband. God uses Nathan to pronounce his judgment on David's family, telling him that "the sword will never depart" from his house because he "despised" the Lord in committing these sins (2 Samuel 12:10). Nathan later ensures that David's son, Solomon, becomes the next king (1 Kings 1).

After Solomon's death, the kingdom of Israel divides into the northern kingdom of Israel and the southern kingdom of Judah,

UNITED

Prophets	Kings
Samuel	Saul, David
Nathan	David, Solomon

NORTHERN KINGDOM

Prophets	Kings
Ahijah	Jeroboam I, Nadab, Baasha, Elah, Zimri, Omri
Elijah, Micaiah	Ahab, Ahaziah
Elijah, Elisha	Joram
Elisha	Jehu, Jehoahaz, Jehoash
Amos, Hosea	Jeroboam II, Zechariah
Hosea	Shallum, Menahem, Pekahiah, Pekah, Hoshea

both ruled by kings with God's appointed prophets by their sides.

The Northern Kingdom (Israel)

Ahijah, appearing around 910 BC, is the first prophet sent to the northern kingdom. He prophesies during the reigns of Israel's first six kings. Ahijah prophesies that Jeroboam will become the king of Israel (1 Kings 11:29–33) and that God will end Jeroboam's lineage because of idol worship under his rule (1 Kings 14:1–19).

Next, during the reign of Ahab, one of Israel's evil kings (1 Kings 16:30), God raises up Elijah, one of Israel's most well-known prophets, in approximately 870 BC. Ahab and his wife Jezebel commit atrocities, such as hunting down and killing the Lord's prophets and leading the Israelites into idol worship which likely involved sexual immorality and child sacrifice (1 Kings 16:30–33; 18:4). Throughout Ahab's reign, Elijah continues to take bold stands against Ahab's actions, prophesying drought, God's judgment, and more, giving Ahab opportunity to repent and turn to God.

Elijah anoints Elisha as his successor in approximately 845 BC. Elisha asks and receives from God "a double portion of the spirit" God gave to Elijah. Elisha prophesies during the reigns of Jehu, Jehoahaz, and Jehoash.

During the reign of Jeroboam II of Israel (which begins in about 790 BC), God raises up the prophets Amos and Hosea. Amos leaves his life as a farmer and shepherd in the southern kingdom of Judah to confront rampant immorality and injustice in Israel. Hosea prophesies during the reigns of the last seven kings of Israel, confronting Israel's unfaithfulness until Israel is overthrown by Assyria and ceases to be a nation (Hosea; 2 Kings 17:1–17).

The Southern Kingdom (Judah)

God also raises up prophets to deliver messages to the southern kingdom of Judah, ruled by David's descendants. The first is Shemaiah, who advises King Rehoboam that the division of the kingdom into Israel and Judah is God's will. Shemaiah warns the king not to fight the Israelites (approximately 930 BC).

God appoints the prophet Joel (in approximately 760 BC) to speak during the reigns of three kings—Joash, Amaziah, and

SOUTHERN KINGDOM

Shemaiah	Rehoboam, Abijah, Asa, Jehoshaphat, Jehoram, Ahaziah, Athaliah (Queen)
Joel, Zechariah	Joash, Amaziah, Uzziah
Isaiah	Uzziah
Isaiah, Micah	Jotham, Ahaz, Hezekiah
Zephaniah, Habakkuk, Jeremiah	Josiah
Jeremiah	Jehoahaz, Jehoiakim
Jeremiah, Ezekiel	Jehoiachin, Zedekiah

Uzziah. Although the time of Joel's ministry is debated, it is likely that he warns the people of Judah of God's impending judgment.

The prophet Isaiah serves during the reigns of Kings Uzziah, Jotham, Ahaz, and Hezekiah (eighth century BC). Micah also prophesies during this period, confronting idolatry in both kingdoms, beginning with the reign of King Jotham in Judah.

Toward the end of Isaiah's and Micah's ministries, Hezekiah becomes king and leads Judah into one of their greatest revivals. During this time, the Assyrian Empire conquers the northern kingdom and threatens Jerusalem in Judah, but Isaiah prophesies that God will drive the invaders off (2 Kings 19). However, when King Hezekiah later allows visiting dignitaries from the distant kingdom of Babylon to see the treasures in the Lord's house, Isaiah rebukes him. Isaiah foretells a time when Babylon will rise to power, conquering Judah and carrying them into captivity (2 Kings 19:14–19).

Between the years of 638 BC and 586 BC God raises up the prophets Zephaniah, Habakkuk, and Jeremiah. This "golden" era includes the reign of the righteous King Josiah, who comes to the throne when he is only eight years old but continually shows that he has a heart to follow the Lord.

Jeremiah's prophetic ministry spans the reigns of four kings—Jehoahaz, Jehoiakim, Jehoaichin, and Zedekiah. When Isaiah's prophesy concerning Babylon's conquest of Judah comes to pass, he warns the people of Judah not to resist God's judgment. Jeremiah prophesies seventy long years of exile in Babylon (Jeremiah 25–29).

Finally, during the reign of the last two kings of Judah before the Babylonian exile, God raises up Ezekiel. He prophesies during the reigns of Jehoiachin and Zedekiah. Ezekiel begins his ministry in Judah, warning the people of the impending destruction of Jerusalem. Even after Jerusalem is captured and Ezekiel is deported to Babylon with his countrymen, he continues to prophesy.

Rulers of Israel & Judah

The royal rulers of Israel and Judah quickly reveal why both nations are exiled; below are the number of good and evil rulers from each kingdom:

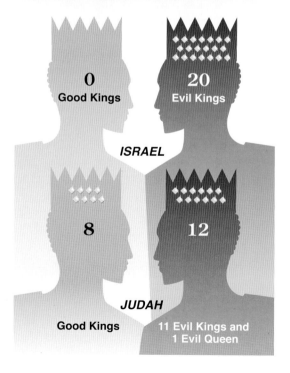

0 Good Kings

20 Evil Kings

ISRAEL

8 Good Kings

12

JUDAH

11 Evil Kings and 1 Evil Queen

FALL OF THE NORTH (ISRAEL)

A rebellion breaks out shortly after Rehoboam is crowned king. He arrogantly rejects the wisdom of the elders and instead follows the advice of young men who instruct him to rule harshly.

Ten tribes rebel and crown Jeroboam as the leader of the northern kingdom of Israel (1 Kings 12:1–20). Under King Jeroboam's rule, the northern kingdom quickly goes astray. He establishes idol worship, reasoning that if the Israelites return to Jerusalem to offer sacrifices to God, they might be tempted to remain there under southern rule. God enacts judgment on Jeroboam through a man named Baasha. Baasha destroys Jeroboam's family and establishes himself as king. He then leads the nation of Israel even further away from God (1 Kings 15:33–34).

Throughout the history of the northern kingdom, God continues to enact judgment on Israel's evil kings for their poor decisions. King Jehu, like all of his successors, does not follow God's commands. Although Jehu purges the kingdom of Baal worship (2 Kings 10:18–30), he continues to allow the worship of other idols. During Jehu's reign, God begins to allow the northern kingdom's enemies to conquer parts of the nation. Instead of relying on the Lord, Israel turns to the surrounding nations for help.

Eventually, King Menahem of Israel pays the Assyrians for their help against enemy nations. Within ten years of forming this alliance, the Assyrians begin to conquer parts of Israel as well. During this time, they deport God's people (2 Kings 15:29), eventually conquering the entire northern kingdom (2 Kings 17:3–23). The northern kingdom of Israel, which exists for just over two centuries, never recovers.

Fall of the Northern Kingdom

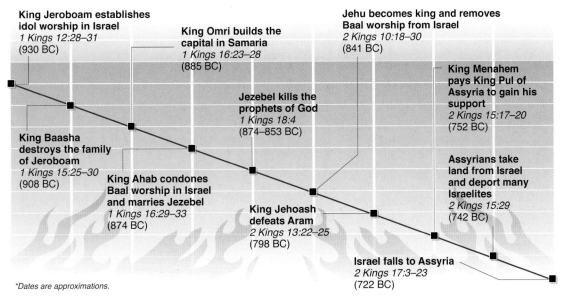

King Jeroboam establishes idol worship in Israel
1 Kings 12:28–31
(930 BC)

King Omri builds the capital in Samaria
1 Kings 16:23–28
(885 BC)

Jehu becomes king and removes Baal worship from Israel
2 Kings 10:18–30
(841 BC)

King Menahem pays King Pul of Assyria to gain his support
2 Kings 15:17–20
(752 BC)

Jezebel kills the prophets of God
1 Kings 18:4
(874–853 BC)

King Baasha destroys the family of Jeroboam
1 Kings 15:25–30
(908 BC)

Assyrians take land from Israel and deport many Israelites
2 Kings 15:29
(742 BC)

King Ahab condones Baal worship in Israel and marries Jezebel
1 Kings 16:29–33
(874 BC)

King Jehoash defeats Aram
2 Kings 13:22–25
(798 BC)

Israel falls to Assyria
2 Kings 17:3–23
(722 BC)

Dates are approximations.

FALL OF THE SOUTH (JUDAH)

When Rehoboam ascends the throne of Israel, a rebellion quickly ensues. Ten tribes of Israel secede to form the northern kingdom of Israel, while two tribes form the southern kingdom of Judah and remain under the rule of David's descendants.

While the northern kingdom is marked by a succession of increasingly evil kings, both good and bad kings lead the southern kingdom. Of the 20 descendants of David who rule Judah, the Bible describes eight as good kings. The southern kingdom experiences revival under the rule of the good kings, but falls back into decline when ruled by kings who do evil in God's sight.

The first revival in the southern kingdom occurs under King Rehoboam's grandson,

King Asa, who "did what was right in the eyes of the LORD, as his father David had done" (1 Kings 15:11). Asa removes the idols made by his ancestors. He even removes his grandmother from her position as queen mother when she makes "a repulsive image for the worship of Asherah" (1 Kings 15:13).

Next in succession is King Jehoshaphat, who continues in his father's ways. However, he makes a fatal decision: he forms a military alliance with Israel's evil King Ahab. Jehoshaphat's son, Jehoram, then goes on to marry Ahab's daughter and begins to worship idols (2 Kings 8:18; 2 Chronicles 21:12–13). The next two kings of the southern kingdom follow in Jehoram's evil ways.

Fall of the Southern Kingdom

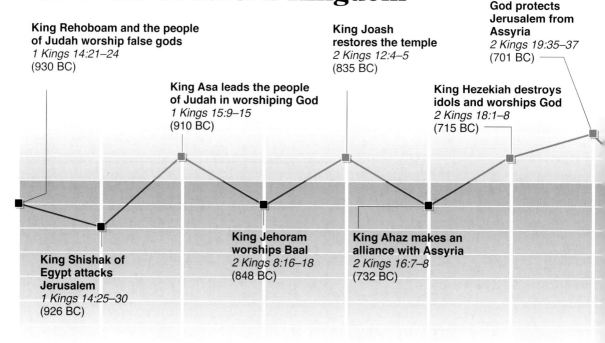

King Rehoboam and the people of Judah worship false gods
1 Kings 14:21–24
(930 BC)

King Asa leads the people of Judah in worshiping God
1 Kings 15:9–15
(910 BC)

King Joash restores the temple
2 Kings 12:4–5
(835 BC)

God protects Jerusalem from Assyria
2 Kings 19:35–37
(701 BC)

King Hezekiah destroys idols and worships God
2 Kings 18:1–8
(715 BC)

King Shishak of Egypt attacks Jerusalem
1 Kings 14:25–30
(926 BC)

King Jehoram worships Baal
2 Kings 8:16–18
(848 BC)

King Ahaz makes an alliance with Assyria
2 Kings 16:7–8
(732 BC)

The kingdom of Judah experiences its longest revival when Joash becomes king. King Joash restores the temple (2 Kings 12:4–5) and begins a 137-year period in which four consecutive kings follow the Lord. Another notable revival is under the leadership of Hezekiah, of whom the Bible says: "There was no one like him among all the kings of Judah, either before him or after him" (2 Kings 18:5).

However, during King Hezekiah's reign, the Assyrians invade Judah twice. During the first invasion, the king of Assyria "exacted from Hezekiah" silver and gold from the Lord's temple (2 Kings 18:14–16). During the Assyrians' second invasion, they directly challenge the ability of the Lord God to save the people of Judah. Facing a much larger enemy army, Hezekiah seeks God. The prophet Isaiah assures him that God will protect Judah. God then routs the Assyrian army by sending an angel to kill 185,000 Assyrians (2 Kings 18–19).

Unfortunately, Hezekiah then makes the poor decision to display the wealth of Judah to visiting emissaries from Babylon. At the time, Babylon is a minor and distant power, but Isaiah prophesies that Judah will eventually be defeated by them and sent into exile there (2 Kings 20:12–19).

Before its downfall, the southern kingdom of Judah experiences one more revival under Hezekiah's great-grandson, Josiah. Josiah becomes king at the age of eight. He is still a young man when he first hears God's law read. Josiah repents and purges Judah of idols (2 Kings 23:1–20). After Josiah is killed in battle, Judah goes into decline. Egypt invades Judah and sets up a puppet king. Later, the Babylonians under Nebuchadnezzar II defeat the Egyptians. Judah becomes a client kingdom of the Babylonian Empire for three years. During this time, the Babylonians deport many of Judah's most promising residents to serve the Babylonian court (2 Kings 24).

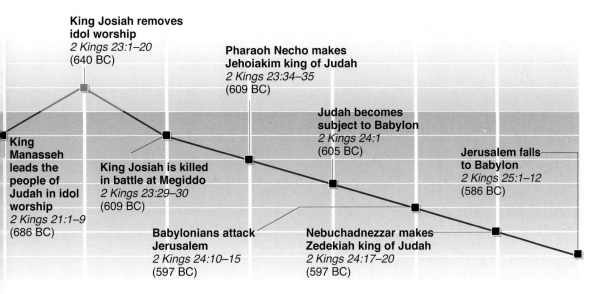

King Josiah removes idol worship
2 Kings 23:1–20
(640 BC)

Pharaoh Necho makes Jehoiakim king of Judah
2 Kings 23:34–35
(609 BC)

Judah becomes subject to Babylon
2 Kings 24:1
(605 BC)

Jerusalem falls to Babylon
2 Kings 25:1–12
(586 BC)

King Manasseh leads the people of Judah in idol worship
2 Kings 21:1–9
(686 BC)

King Josiah is killed in battle at Megiddo
2 Kings 23:29–30
(609 BC)

Babylonians attack Jerusalem
2 Kings 24:10–15
(597 BC)

Nebuchadnezzar makes Zedekiah king of Judah
2 Kings 24:17–20
(597 BC)

LIFE IN EXILE

The province of Babylon overthrows the Assyrian Empire, which has ruled over them for nearly 300 years. When the new Babylonian Empire conquers the Assyrians, they assume control over the northern kingdom of Israel. Seven years later, the Babylonians invade the southern kingdom of Judah.

The Babylonians' initial foray into Judah results in the kingdom of Judah becoming a client kingdom of Babylon, forced to pay tribute and accept the position of a vassal state (2 Kings 24:1). During this time, Babylon deports members of the noble families of Judah (2 Kings 23:29 – 25:21). Daniel, a young man who later becomes a prophet, goes to Babylon with the first wave of exiles.

For three years, the southern kingdom of Judah submits to Babylonian rule. Then, despite warnings from the prophet Jeremiah that God's people would be exiled to Babylon for seventy years, King Jehoiakim of Judah allies himself with Egypt and other neighboring client-kingdoms. Together, they rebel against the Babylonians (2 Kings 24:1 – 7; Jeremiah 44:11 – 14).

Nebuchadnezzar besieges Jerusalem, halting the uprising. The Babylonians steal the temple's treasure, fulfilling Isaiah's prophecy (2 Kings 20:14 – 19).

After subduing Judah, the Babylonians deport more of God's people. This second group of exiles includes King Jehoiachin and his family (2 Kings 24:15). It also includes Ezekiel, a priest who becomes one of the most significant prophets to preach during the exile (Ezekiel 1:1 – 3). The deportation also includes all of Jerusalem's craftsmen and military leaders. Only the poorest

Life in Exile

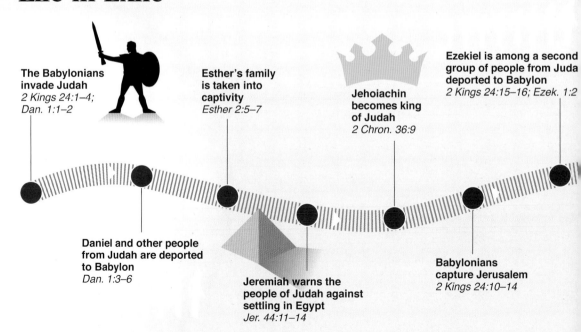

The Babylonians invade Judah
2 Kings 24:1–4;
Dan. 1:1–2

Esther's family is taken into captivity
Esther 2:5–7

Jehoiachin becomes king of Judah
2 Chron. 36:9

Ezekiel is among a second group of people from Juda deported to Babylon
2 Kings 24:15–16; Ezek. 1:2

Daniel and other people from Judah are deported to Babylon
Dan. 1:3–6

Jeremiah warns the people of Judah against settling in Egypt
Jer. 44:11–14

Babylonians capture Jerusalem
2 Kings 24:10–14

inhabitants are left behind (2 Kings 24:14). Nebuchadnezzar appoints Jehoiachin's uncle, Zedekiah, as client king over Judah (2 Kings 24:17).

After nine years serving as a vassal king, Zedekiah rebels. In response, Nebuchadnezzar besieges Jerusalem for almost two years. This leads to famine and deprivation within the city. Ultimately, the Babylonians breach Jerusalem's walls. They destroy the walls and burn down the Lord's temple, the palace, and large parts of the city. They deport all of Jerusalem's residents except for a few farmers (2 Kings 25:1–21; Jeremiah 52:12–14).

Sixty-six years into the exile period, the Persian Empire under Cyrus II conquers Babylon and assumes rule over both the exiles and the province of Judah. Early in his reign, Cyrus issues a decree allowing the Jews and other captive peoples to return to their homeland (Ezra 1:1–4).

Some of the Jewish people return to Judah, while others remain in Babylon. During this time, the Jewish people still face periodic persecution. In one instance, a young Jewish woman named Esther is chosen by King Xerxes, one of Cyrus II's successors, to become queen of Persia. She uses her position and her power to save the Jewish people from being annihilated.

God's people who return to Jerusalem eventually rebuild the city's walls and the temple, despite considerable opposition from the rulers of rival provinces (as recorded in the Bible books of Ezra and Nehemiah). Other Israelites choose to remain in Babylon and other parts of the Persian Empire.

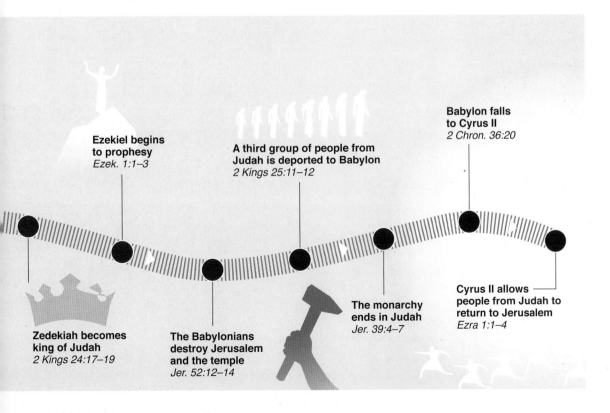

Ezekiel begins to prophesy
Ezek. 1:1–3

A third group of people from Judah is deported to Babylon
2 Kings 25:11–12

Babylon falls to Cyrus II
2 Chron. 36:20

The monarchy ends in Judah
Jer. 39:4–7

Cyrus II allows people from Judah to return to Jerusalem
Ezra 1:1–4

Zedekiah becomes king of Judah
2 Kings 24:17–19

The Babylonians destroy Jerusalem and the temple
Jer. 52:12–14

RETURN AND REBUILDING

God ends the period of Jewish exile in Babylonia by moving the heart of King Cyrus of Persia. In his first year as king, Cyrus issues a proclamation allowing the Jews to return to the land of Judah and rebuild the temple in Jerusalem. Fulfilling a prophecy of Jeremiah, this decree comes after the Jews have been living in captivity for 70 years. King Cyrus provides for the return of the 5,400 gold and silver temple articles that Babylon had stolen (see 2 Chronicles 36:22–23; Ezra 1).

Cyrus's royal decree states that any of the Jewish people within the Persian Empire may return to Judah. In addition, he decrees that the people of the lands that God's people live in are to supply the returning exiles with gold, silver, livestock, and other goods (Ezra 1:2–4). In the first trip, nearly 50,000 Jews return to Jerusalem, including priests, musicians, temple gatekeepers, slaves, and descendants of the royal line of Solomon (Ezra 2:64–65).

Upon their return,

God's people present an offering to God for the temple's rebuilding at the site of the original temple. Nearly seven months later, the returned exiles rebuild the altar where the original altar first stood (Ezra 3:2–6). As they lay the temple's foundation, all of the people sing praise to God (Ezra 3:7–13). In fact, those who are old enough to have seen

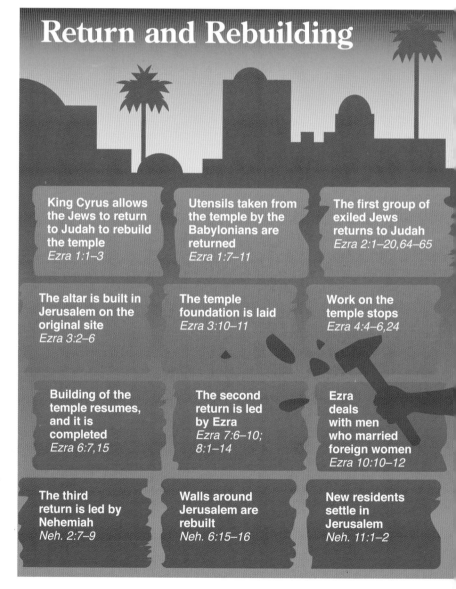

Return and Rebuilding

King Cyrus allows the Jews to return to Judah to rebuild the temple
Ezra 1:1–3

Utensils taken from the temple by the Babylonians are returned
Ezra 1:7–11

The first group of exiled Jews returns to Judah
Ezra 2:1–20,64–65

The altar is built in Jerusalem on the original site
Ezra 3:2–6

The temple foundation is laid
Ezra 3:10–11

Work on the temple stops
Ezra 4:4–6,24

Building of the temple resumes, and it is completed
Ezra 6:7,15

The second return is led by Ezra
Ezra 7:6–10; 8:1–14

Ezra deals with men who married foreign women
Ezra 10:10–12

The third return is led by Nehemiah
Neh. 2:7–9

Walls around Jerusalem are rebuilt
Neh. 6:15–16

New residents settle in Jerusalem
Neh. 11:1–2

the first temple weep loudly and shout for joy, celebrating the restoration of Jerusalem and God's temple (Ezra 3:12–13).

Just when things seem to be coming together, the enemies of Judah offer to help the Jews rebuild the temple. They claim that they also worship the Lord God. However, when the people of Judah refuse their help, these enemies interfere with the rebuilding effort by bribing Persian officials. As a result, the temple rebuilding ceases for more than 50 years (Ezra 4:1–5).

The temple's construction resumes during the reign of Cyrus's great-grandson, King Darius. When Darius discovers a scroll containing Cyrus's order to have the temple rebuilt, he issues his own decree: that anyone who opposes the rebuilding of the temple will be killed (Ezra 6:6–12). Work then resumes until the temple is completely rebuilt (Ezra 6:14–15).

After Darius dies, he is succeeded by his son, Ahasuerus, also called Xerxes. King Xerxes eventually chooses Esther, one of the Jews who have remained in Babylon, as his queen. Esther is instrumental in establishing the favorable treatment of the Jews during Xerxes' rein.

When Esther's stepson is king of Persia, a second group of exiled Jews returns to Judah, led by Ezra, a Jewish scribe and priest (Ezra 7–8). Ezra reestablishes the importance of God's law in the hearts of the people of Judah. One of the ways he does this is through commanding men who have broken God's law by marrying foreign women to separate from their foreign wives (Ezra 10:10–12).

Roughly ten years after Ezra leads the

Opposition to Rebuilding
Ezra 4:12–22

The Samaritans file a vindictive report to the king of Persia that claims the following:

Jerusalem is a wicked city

Jerusalem will stop paying taxes

Jerusalem is troublesome to kings and provinces

Jerusalem has a long history of revolt and sedition

Jerusalem is a threat to royal interests

© Zondervan. Used by permission

second group of exiles to Judah, Nehemiah leaves a position of trust and authority in Babylon to lead a third group of exiles back to Jerusalem. Nehemiah is concerned that the city's walls have not been rebuilt, leaving Jerusalem an easy target for invaders.

Nehemiah then leads God's people in the rebuilding of Jerusalem's wall, despite opposition from rivals in neighboring provinces (Nehemiah 6:15–16). When the walls are rebuilt, the exiles are settled, with 10 percent living in Jerusalem while the other 90 percent reside in neighboring towns and nearby cities (Nehemiah 11:1–2). At this point, the successful reestablishment of God's people seems possible.

ESTHER'S STORY

Even though God's name is not mentioned once in the book of Esther, his provision for his people, the Jews, is evident. Esther's story begins when Queen Vashti refuses a request from her husband, King Xerxes, to appear before the people wearing her crown to show off her beauty (Esther 1:9–12). The king is angry about being publicly insulted by his wife, and his advisors recommend divorcing her (Esther 1:19–22), reasoning that Queen Vashti's act could set a precedent for disobedience among other wives throughout the land.

King Xerxes orders Vashti to be put away according to the laws of the Medes and the Persians—laws that cannot legally be altered by anyone once the king has decreed them. Afterward, his advisors suggest holding a beauty contest to choose Queen Vashti's replacement. Esther, a young Jewish woman living with her uncle, Mordecai, is selected for the king's contest. She is put into the king's harem and given beauty treatments for a full year in anticipation of spending a single night with the king. Like the other women chosen to spend a night with the king, Esther will spend the rest of her life in the harem with the king's concubines unless Xerxes asks for her company.

Upon her uncle's suggestion, Esther is careful not to reveal that she is Jewish. This stealthy approach is likely taken because many within the Persian Empire are offended by the Jews' refusal to worship or bow to anyone but the one true God.

After her year of preparation, Esther spends her night with the king. He is pleased with her and names her queen in Vashti's place.

Sometime after Esther becomes queen, a high-ranking Persian official named Haman takes offense at Mordecai's refusal to bow before him. Haman decides to persuade the king to eradicate all of the Jews in retribution. He offers the king 750,000 pounds of silver to issue a decree ordering the execution of the Jews. The king agrees and issues the decree (Esther 3).

When Mordecai hears of the plan to kill the Jews, he passes a note to Esther. He informs her of the plot against the Jews, warning her that it will affect her, even though she is queen. He challenges her, "For if you remain silent at this time, relief and deliverance for the Jews will arise from another place ... and who knows but that you have come to your royal position for such a time as this?" (Esther 4:14). Esther takes Mordecai's request to heart, asking the Jews to pray and fast for her.

Appearing before the king without being summoned is punishable by death, but after fasting and praying, Esther boldly takes her life in her hands for the sake of her people. She approaches the throne. The king is pleased with her and spares her, promising to give her whatever she asks for. She asks him to bring Haman and attend a banquet, which she will prepare (Esther 5:1–5).

At the banquet, the king repeats his promise to give Esther whatever she requests. Esther requests that the king bring Haman again and attend another banquet she will host the next night (Esther 5:6–8). Haman soaks in the sense of being honored but is still unhappy because Mordecai continues to refuse to bow to him (Esther 5:9–14).

That night, the king is unable to sleep.

He learns from having accounts of history read to him that nothing has been done to honor Mordecai for averting an assassination attempt on him years earlier. Xerxes asks Haman how he should honor someone. Thinking he is the one to be honored, Haman suggests robing the individual and leading him through the city on a horse. Haman is then humiliated when he has to implement this very plan for Mordecai (Esther 6).

That night at the feast, the king again promises to give Esther whatever she asks for. Esther then reveals that she is Jewish and that Haman is plotting to kill her and her people. The king is furious and has Haman hanged on a gallows Haman had constructed to hang Mordecai on. The king cannot legally undo the decree he signed for the execution of the Jews, but he issues a new decree allowing the Jews to defend themselves from arrest and execution using deadly force (Esther 8:11).

The king further appoints Mordecai as his second in command, putting him in a good position to benefit the other Jews (Esther 10). These events lead many of the people of other nationalities within the Persian Empire to convert to Judaism (Esther 8:17) and leads to the establishment of the Jewish Feast of Purim, a celebration of deliverance (Esther 9).

Numbers in the Book of Esther

0 **God is mentioned in the book**
Number of times

Number of pounds of silver Haman contributes to the royal treasury in exchange for Xerxes' decree against the Jews:
750,000

Number of years Esther is queen before Haman's plot against the Jews is finalized:
☒☒☒☒☒☒☒☒ **8**

Number of years covered in this book: **10**
☒☒☒☒☒☒☒☒☒☒

Number of miles between Susa and Jerusalem:
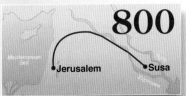
800
Jerusalem • • Susa

2 Number of days involved in Esther's banquets for Xerxes:

75 Number of feet spanning the pole Haman sets up in order to hang Mordecai

POINTING TO THE MESSIAH

Long before Jesus comes into this world to save us from our sin, God's people look forward to a coming Messiah, a Deliverer who will free them from Roman rule. Jesus' coming, however, defies their expectations. The Messianic prophecies reveal God's greater plan to deliver the entire world.

Seven centuries before Jesus is born, Isaiah tells God's people that their Savior will be born of a chosen young woman, a virgin (Isaiah 7:14, fulfilled in Matthew 1:20–23). The prophet Micah, a contemporary of Isaiah's, foretells Jesus' place of birth, the small, otherwise insignificant town of Bethlehem in Judea (Micah 5:2, fulfilled in Matthew 2:1–6).

The prophets Isaiah and Malachi both proclaim that there will be a forerunner who will prepare the way for the Messiah (Isaiah 40:3; Malachi 3:1). These prophecies are fulfilled by John the Baptist, who is the first to reveal to the people that Jesus is the Deliverer God has sent (John 1:29–34). Jesus personally affirms the fact that John fulfills these prophecies (Matthew 11:7–10).

Isaiah 61 foretells the Messiah preaching the good news of God's kingdom. Jesus reads this passage aloud in the synagogue and shocks those in his hometown when he claims that this prophecy is being fulfilled in their presence (Luke 4:16–21, 43–44). Other aspects of his earthly ministry foretold by Old Testament prophets include the expectation that the Messiah comes to save his people (Ezekiel 34:12, 16, fulfilled in Luke 19:10). Jesus' healing ministry matches Isaiah's description of God saving his people (Isaiah 35:5–6, fulfilled in Matthew 11:4–6). The psalmist indicates that God's servant uses parables to teach his people (Psalm 78:1–2, fulfilled in Matthew 13:34–35; Luke 14–16; and elsewhere).

Just as the details of Jesus' life, teaching, miracles, and ministry are foretold by prophecy, so are the details surrounding his death. Prophesying after the rebuilding of the temple, Zechariah foretells that God's servant will be rejected by God's people (Zechariah 11:13). Judas Iscariot fulfills this prophecy when he leads a mob to Jesus and betrays the Lord with a kiss (Luke 22:47–48). The prophet Zechariah even details how much money the Lord's enemies will pay his betrayer and what the betrayer will ultimately do with the money (Zechariah 11:12–13, fulfilled in Matthew 26:14–16; 27:3–10).

In addition to many direct prophecies in the Bible, many stories in the Old Testament foreshadow the life and ministry of Christ.

After Jesus rises from the dead, he shows his disciples—who are still in mourning—why his death was necessary and how his death and resurrection fulfill the Scriptures (Luke 24:25–27; Romans 6:4–5; 1 Corinthians 15:3–5).

Paul claims that Jesus fulfills the Psalm 68:18 promise that the Messiah will "ascend on high" in his letter to the Ephesians (Ephesians 4:8–10). After Jesus ascends to heaven, an angel tells the astonished disciples that he will return in the same way they saw him ascend. Since then, believers await Jesus' return in fulfillment of prophecy.

Messianic Hopes

Jesus' Birth

PRECEDED BY A MESSENGER:
Isa. 40:3; Mal. 3:1;
fulfilled in Matt. 11:10; Mark 1:1–3

BORN OF A VIRGIN:
Isa. 7:14; fulfilled in Matt. 1:20–23

BORN IN BETHLEHEM:
Micah 5:2; fulfilled in Matt. 2:1–2

PRESENTED AS GOD'S FIRSTBORN SON:
Exod. 13:12–13;
fulfilled in Luke 2:6–7,22–23

Old Testament books with prophecies about Christ:

23

Jesus has fulfilled every Messianic prophecy with

100% accuracy

Jesus' Teaching

PREACHES THE GOOD NEWS OF GOD'S KINGDOM:
Isa. 61:1–3;
fulfilled in Luke 4:16–21,43–44

USES PARABLES:
Psalm 78:1–2;
fulfilled in Matt. 13:34–35

Jesus' Ministry

HAS COME TO SAVE PEOPLE:
Ezek. 34:12,16; fulfilled in Luke 19:10

PERFORMS MIRACLES TO SHOW HE IS GOD:
Isa. 35:5–6; fulfilled in Matt. 11:4–6

Jesus' Last Hours Before Death

PIERCED IN HIS HANDS AND SIDE:
Zech. 12:10;
fulfilled in John 19:34; 20:27

BREAKS NO BONES:
Num. 9:12; Psalm 34:20;
fulfilled in John 19:33,36

BETRAYED BY A FRIEND:
Psalm 41:9; fulfilled in
John 13:18,21–30

Psalm 22:1–18

Foreshadows Jesus' crucifixion

Jesus quotes *22:1*

while hanging on the cross:
Matt. 27:46; Mark 15:34

40 Days

Jesus fasts in the wilderness

Jesus remains on earth after his resurrection

Jesus' Resurrection

DIES AND RISES AGAIN:
Job 19:23–27; Hosea 6:2; fulfilled in
Luke 24:46; Rom. 6:4–5,9; 1 Cor. 15:3–5;
Phil. 3:10; 1 Peter 1:3

ASCENDS TO HEAVEN:
Psalms 47:5; 68:18; fulfilled in Eph. 4:8–10

BIRTH AND BAPTISM OF CHRIST

Before Jesus is born, God sends the angel Gabriel to Zechariah, an elderly priest. The angel tells him that his wife, Elizabeth, is going to have a baby who will "make ready a people prepared for the Lord" (Luke 1:17). This baby is John the Baptist. Then, God sends Gabriel to Elizabeth's cousin, a young virgin named Mary who is engaged to a carpenter named Joseph. Gabriel tells her that the Holy Spirit will come upon her and that she will conceive a child who will be called "the Son of the Most High" (Luke 1:32, 35).

When Joseph learns that Mary is pregnant, he intends to break their engagement quietly. He changes his mind and marries her when an angel appears to him in a dream. The angel cites Isaiah's prophecy that "'the virgin will conceive and give birth to a son, and they will call him Immanuel'

(which means 'God with us')" (Matthew 1:18–24, quoting Isaiah 7:14).

When Mary is almost ready to give birth, she and Joseph must travel to Bethlehem in order to participate in a Roman census. When they arrive in Bethlehem, there is not enough room for all of the travelers in the inns. Mary gives birth to Jesus in a stable. Then, the angel of the Lord appears to shepherds in a nearby field, saying: "I bring you good news that will cause great joy for all the people. Today in the town of David a Savior has been born to you; he is the Messiah, the Lord" (Luke 2:10–11).

Around the age of thirty, Jesus launched his public ministry by being baptized by his cousin—John the Baptist (Matthew 3:15–17). John is an eccentric preacher who wears garments similar to those worn

Birth of Christ

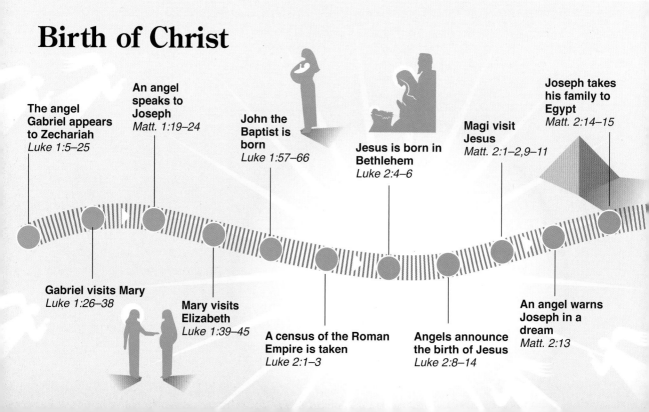

The angel Gabriel appears to Zechariah
Luke 1:5–25

An angel speaks to Joseph
Matt. 1:19–24

John the Baptist is born
Luke 1:57–66

Jesus is born in Bethlehem
Luke 2:4–6

Magi visit Jesus
Matt. 2:1–2,9–11

Joseph takes his family to Egypt
Matt. 2:14–15

Gabriel visits Mary
Luke 1:26–38

Mary visits Elizabeth
Luke 1:39–45

A census of the Roman Empire is taken
Luke 2:1–3

Angels announce the birth of Jesus
Luke 2:8–14

An angel warns Joseph in a dream
Matt. 2:13

by the prophet Elijah (2 Kings 1:8; Mark 1:6). His diet consists of locusts and honey, which was standard fare for the poor (Matthew 3:4).

The baptism John offered may have been a public ritual cleansing that was often encouraged in the Pentateuch (Exodus 19:10–11; Leviticus 6:28; 11:28, 40; 13). Urging people to cleanse themselves from their lives of sin, John provided a ritual cleansing to symbolize the forgiveness of God.

Because John knows of Jesus' special nature (John 1:29), he objects to the idea of baptizing Jesus and tries to refuse Jesus' request (Matthew 3:14). Jesus persuades him to continue and launches his ministry with a public display of God's approval when a voice speaks from heaven: "This is my Son, whom I love; with him I am well pleased" (Matthew 3:17).

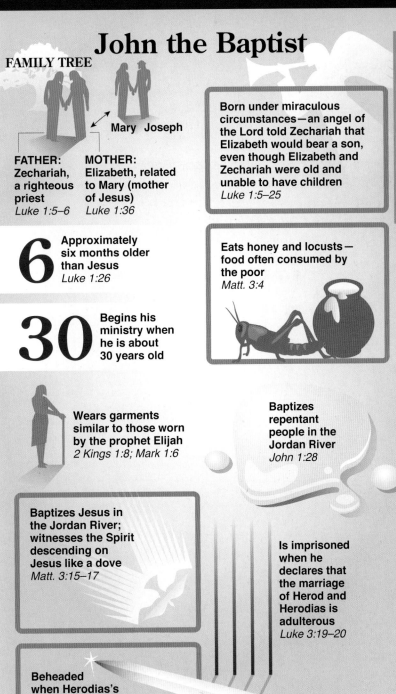

John the Baptist

EVENTS AND STORY LINE

FAMILY TREE

Mary   Joseph

FATHER: Zechariah, a righteous priest
Luke 1:5–6

MOTHER: Elizabeth, related to Mary (mother of Jesus)
Luke 1:36

Born under miraculous circumstances—an angel of the Lord told Zechariah that Elizabeth would bear a son, even though Elizabeth and Zechariah were old and unable to have children
Luke 1:5–25

6 Approximately six months older than Jesus
Luke 1:26

Eats honey and locusts—food often consumed by the poor
Matt. 3:4

30 Begins his ministry when he is about 30 years old

Wears garments similar to those worn by the prophet Elijah
2 Kings 1:8; Mark 1:6

Baptizes repentant people in the Jordan River
John 1:28

Baptizes Jesus in the Jordan River; witnesses the Spirit descending on Jesus like a dove
Matt. 3:15–17

Is imprisoned when he declares that the marriage of Herod and Herodias is adulterous
Luke 3:19–20

Beheaded when Herodias's daughter Salome asks Herod for his head
Mark 6:14–19

TEACHINGS OF JESUS

The Gospels record Jesus teaching on a variety of topics centered on the kingdom of God. In the kingdom that Jesus speaks of, one does not enter by being perfect but by believing in the promises of God. Jesus states, "Unless your righteousness surpasses that of the Pharisees and the teachers of the law, you will certainly not enter the kingdom of heaven" (Matthew 5:20). Since we clearly cannot surpass the righteousness of the Pharisees, Jesus teaches that we practice a purer devotion to God when we rely on faith rather than performance.

Throughout the three years of his ministry, Jesus goes about proclaiming in word and deed that the kingdom of God is "at hand." His teachings are always amplified by his actions. He not only preaches mercy; he shows mercy to "the least of these" and calls his true followers to do the same (Matthew 25:40). Jesus is constantly willing to break social barriers to show love to all people, even reaching out to Samaritans, who are despised by the Jewish people at the time.

Jesus' teaching methods share some similarities to the popular moral philosophies of his time and to later rabbinic writings. However, there isn't enough evidence to demonstrate that Jesus is following any specific method, be it Jewish or GrecoRoman. The Gospels are careful to indicate that Jesus' teachings come from his special relationship with God, so Jesus does not follow any form of education that we can identify. He is a teacher of wisdom, and as such he is similar with other teachers in at least one significant way: he asks thoughtprovoking questions to drive certain teachings. For example, he asks, "Can any one of you by worrying add a single hour to your life?" (Matthew 6:27).

Some of Jesus' teachings seem radical and impossible to follow apart from the power of God through the Holy Spirit. In one instance, a Jewish leader seeks Jesus' insight on an aspect of the law. He inquires about how to inherit eternal life. Jesus, seeing the man's heart, understands the grip of wealth on him and challenges him, "Sell everything you have and give to the poor, and you will have treasure in heaven. Then come, follow me." The young leader becomes sad because of his great wealth. Jesus then turns to the crowd, stating: "What is impossible with man is possible with God" (Luke 18:18–29).

What often most irritated the Jewish leaders of Jesus' day is what Jesus taught and said about himself. He claimed he was the only way to God (John 14:6). He publicly stated his ability to forgive sins (Luke 5:20–21) and give eternal life (John 11:25). He even claimed to exist before Abraham (John 8:58) and promised to return as the judge of the world (Matthew 25:31–32)

Most importantly, Jesus' life reveals the heart of love that the Father has for a fallen humanity. Jesus, reflecting the Father's heart, is "moved with compassion" when he sees people suffering. In interaction with other people, Jesus displays God's great kindness. During his life he frees hurting people from the bondage of sickness, death, and the demonic. Finally, in the work of the cross, Jesus frees all who believe in him from the power of sin and death (Romans 5:17).

THE NUMBER OF PARABLES IN EACH GOSPEL:

Luke — 28
Matthew — 23
Mark — 9
John — 0

TALK, TOUCH OR SPIT?

▶ Jesus heals people in three primary ways throughout the Gospels.

THE NUMBER OF TIMES JESUS PERFORMS EACH METHOD OF HEALING:

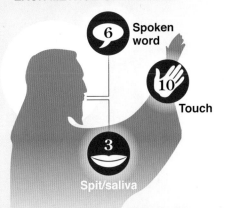

6 — Spoken word
10 — Touch
3 — Spit/saliva

THE OPPOSITION

THE NUMBER OF TIMES THE RELIGIOUS LEADERS ACCUSE, CRITICIZE AND QUESTION JESUS IN THE GOSPELS:

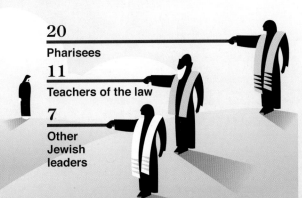

20 Pharisees
11 Teachers of the law
7 Other Jewish leaders

THE NUMBER OF QUESTIONS JESUS ASKS IN THE GOSPELS:

343

BREAKING BARRIERS

▶ Because the Jewish people of Jesus' day did not intentionally mingle with Gentiles, Jesus' loving interaction with them stood out to everyone.

THE NUMBER OF TIMES JESUS INTERACTS WITH GENTILES IN THE GOSPELS:

 4 — Gentiles follow and speak to Jesus

 4 — Gentiles are healed by Jesus

 2 — Gentiles are delivered from demons by Jesus

CRITICISM AND QUESTIONS

THE NUMBER OF TIMES JESUS ENDURES CRITICISM AND QUESTIONING BY RELIGIOUS LEADERS IN THE GOSPELS:

Questioned about his authority
— 12

Criticized for healing or working on the Sabbath
— 5

Criticized for socializing with sinners
— 4

Questioned regarding matters of the law
— 4

Here is a list of topics and references Jesus taught on:

Adultery and Marriage   Matthew 5:27–32; 19:4–8; Luke 16:18

Children   Matthew 19:13–15; Mark 9:36–37; 10:13–16; Luke 18:15–17

Church and Church Discipline   Matthew 16:17–20; 18:15 –18; 21:12–13; Mark 11:17; Luke 18:45–46

Communion   Matthew 26:26–29; Mark 14:22–25; Luke 22:17–23

Divorce   Matthew 5:31–32; 19:3–12; Mark 10:2–12

Doing God's Will   Matthew 7:21–27; 10:40–42; 12:48–50; 21:28–32; 25:1–13, 34–36, 40; 26:39; Mark 3:33–35; 9:37; Luke 6:46–49; 8:16–18; 12:47–48; John 6:28–29, 38–40; 10:17–18

Faith   Matthew 9:22, 29; 8:13; 15:24–28; 17:20; 21:21–22; Mark 11:22–23; Luke 7:50; 17:6

Fasting   Matthew 6:16–18; Mark 2:18–21; Luke 5:34

Following Christ and Being His Disciple   Matthew 8:20–22; 10:34–39; 28–30; 16:24–26; 19:21, 28–30; Mark 1:17; 8:34–38; Luke 9:23–26, 57–62; 10:1–12, 16, 18–20; 14:25–35; John 8:12, 31–32; 12:25–26; 14:12

Forgiveness   Matthew 6:14; 18:21–35; Mark 11:25; Luke 6:37; 7:41–42; 17:3–4

Forgiveness of Sins   Matthew 9:4–6, 12–13; Mark 2:8–12; Luke 5:22–24; 7:44–49; John 8:34–36

Fulfilling of the Law   Matthew 5:17–20; 7:12; 8:4; 9:14–17; 15:3–6, 10–11; 22:37–40; Luke 16:16–17

Giving   Matthew 6:2–4; Mark 12:41–46; Luke 6:29–30, 38; 21:1–4

His Death on the Cross   Matthew 17:12–13, 22–23; 20:17–19; 21:33–45; 26:1–2, 11–13; Mark 9:31; 10:32–34; John 12:23–24, 31–32

His Deity   Matthew 22:42–45; 28:18; John 8:58; 9:35–37; 10:25–30, 38; 12:44–46; 14:6–7, 9–11; 16:26

Human Heart   Matthew 13:1–9, 18–23; 15:16–20; Mark 4:3–8, 13–19; 7:14–23; Luke 6:43–45; 8:4–8, 11–15

Humility   Matthew 5:3, 5; 11:25; 18:2–5; 20:26–28; 23:8–12; Mark 9:35; 10:15; Luke 9:47–48; 14:7–11; 18:9–14

Hypocrisy of Pharisees   Matthew 6:2, 5; 23:1–7, 13–33; Mark 7:9–13; 12:38–40; Luke 11:37–44; 12:1–3; 18:9–14; 20:45–47; John 5:37b–44

Identity in Christ   Matthew 5:13–16; Mark 9:49–50

Judging Others   Matthew 7:1–5; Luke 6:37–38, 41–42

Judgment   Matthew 5:21–22; 13:40–42, 47–50; 18:6–9; 21:42–45; 22:11–14; 24:48–51; 25:28–30, 31–46; Mark 9:41–48; Luke 6:24–25; 10:13–15; 11:47–50; 13:22–30; 20:9–19; John 9:39; 12:47–50

Kingdom of God/Heaven   Matthew 5:3, 10; 6:33; 11:4–11; 13:31–33, 44–48; 19:14, 23; 20:1–16; 22:1–14; Mark 4:26–29, 30–32; 13:18–21; 14:15–24; John 14:1–4

Kingdom of God Versus Kingdom of Darkness Matthew 3:24–27; 12:25–30; 13:24–30, 37–43; Luke 11:14–23

Lack of Repentance Matthew 11:20–24; 12:39–42, 43–45; 21:32

Last Days/The End of the Age Matthew 13:27–30, 36–43, 47–50; 19:28–30; 24:4–14, 32–35; Mark 13:5–8, 14–25; Luke 12:54–56; 17:28–35; 21:8–11, 20–31

Love Matthew 5:43–44, 46; 22:37–40; Mark 12:29–31; Luke 6:27–36; 10:27; John 3:16; 14:20–21, 23–24; 15:9–17

The Lost Matthew 18:12–14; Mark 2:15–17; Luke 15:1–31; 18:9–14

Making Oath Matthew 5:33–37

Mercy Matthew 5:7; 9:12–13; Luke 6:36; 10:33–37

Multiplying the Gifts Matthew 25:14–30; Luke 19:11–27

Murder Matthew 5:21–22a

Persecution Matthew 5:10–12; 10:16–24, 26–31; Mark 13:8, 12–13; Luke 6:22–23; 21:12–19; John 15:18–25; 16:1–4

Prayer Matthew 5:44; 6:5–13; 7:7–11; 9:38; 18:19–20; Mark 9:28–29; 11:24; Luke 6:28; 11:2–13; 18:1–8; John 14:13–14; 15:7; 16:23–24

Purity of the Heart Matthew 5:8; 6:22–23; 13:16–17; Luke 11:33–36

Readiness Matthew 24:42–51; 25:1–13; 26:38; 40–41; Mark 13:32–37; 14:37–38; Luke 12:35–40

Reconciliation Matthew 5:9, 23–26; Luke 12:57–59

Righteousness Matthew 5:6, 20; 6:1, 33

Rejection of Christ Matthew 21:33–42; 26:34; Mark 12:1–11

Repentance Matthew 4:17; 5:4; Mark 1:15; Luke 13:1–9

Respecting Authority Matthew 17:24–27; 22:15–22; Mark 12:17; Luke 20:20–25

Resurrection Matthew 22:29–32; Mark 9:31; 12:24–27; Luke 20:27–38; John 5:25–32; 6:39–40; 11:25

Rest and Peace Matthew 11:28–30; John 16:33

Sabbath Matthew 12:3–7, 11–12; Mark 2:27; Luke 6:1–10; 13:15–16; John 7:21–24

Second Coming and Great Tribulation Matthew 16:27–28; 23:37–39; 24:15–25, 26–31, 32–34, 36–39; 25:1–28; Mark 13:26–27, 14–25; Luke 17:20–35

Serving Matthew 20:26–28; Mark 9:35; 10:42–45; Luke 7:36–46; 10:30–35; 17:7–10; 21:24–30; John 8:9–11, 4–36

Sin Matthew 12:31–32; 15:16–20; 18:15–17; Mark 3:28–29; Luke 12:10; 17:1–4

Spiritual Blindness Matthew 13:13–15; 15:13–14; 16:2–4, 8–12; 22:16–26; Mark 4:11–12; 7:6–8; 8:17–20

True and False Prophets Matthew 7:15–20; 12:33–37; Luke 2:26; John 10:1, 8

True Family Matthew 12:49–50; Mark 3:33–35; 10:29–31; Luke 8:19–21

True Riches/Treasures Matthew 6:19–21; 13:52; 19:21; Mark 10:21; Luke 12:32–34; 14:12–14; 18:18–30

Witnessing Matthew 4:19; 9:37–38; 10:5–32; 28:18–20; Mark 6:9–11; 13:10–11; 16:15–18; Luke 9:3–6; 12:8–9

Not Worrying Matthew 6:25–34; Luke 12:22–31

MIRACLES OF CHRIST

EVENTS AND STORY LINE

Because he is the Son of the living God, Jesus' person and ministry mark the beginning of God's kingdom on earth. He comes to proclaim the good news, that God has sent his Son into the world, not to condemn the world, but to save the world (John 3:16–17). As a sign of the beginning of God's reign on earth, Jesus' ministry is identified by many signs and wonders, or miraculous events that cannot be explained by any natural causes.

When John the Baptist sends his followers to ask Jesus whether he is the promised Messiah, Jesus points to the miraculous:

"Go back and report to John what you have seen and heard: The blind receive sight, the lame walk, those who have leprosy are cleansed, the deaf hear, the dead are raised, and the good news is proclaimed to the poor" (Luke 7:22).

Jesus ushers in a new world order. When Jesus calms a storm, he reveals both his authority over nature and a coming reality in which nature will no longer have the power to devastate or destroy. When Jesus restores an outcast woman's body to health and commands the crippled to walk, he reveals both his authority over sickness and a coming reality in which our bodies will not suffer from disease or death. His miracles reveal God's mercy.

Jesus' miracles provide a foretaste of the goodness of God's unfolding plan, a restored heaven and earth (Revelation 21–22). Jesus, the coming King, will one day make *all* things new (Revelation 21:5).

The Gospels record about 40 miracles of Jesus:

Miracles of Christ

The Gospels record more than 40 stories involving Jesus performing miracles

Healing People — **20**

Freeing People Affected by Demons — **11**

Excercising Authority over Nature — **10**

Raising the Dead — **3**

Healing People

- Leper (Matthew 8:1–3)
- Centurion's servant (Matthew 8:5–13)
- Peter's mother-in-law (Matthew 8:14–15)
- Many sick people (Matthew 8:16)
- Paralytic (Matthew 9:2–8)
- Bleeding woman (Matthew 9:20–22)
- Two blind men (Matthew 9:27–30)
- Shriveled hand (Matthew 12:9–14)
- Many healed at Gennesaret (Matthew 14:34–36)

- Many others healed (Matthew 15:29–31)
- Two blind men healed (Matthew 20:29–34)
- Deaf and mute man (Mark 7:31–35)
- Blind man at Bethsaida (Mark 8:22–26)
- Crippled woman (Luke 13:10–13)
- Man with a swelling (Luke 14:1–4)
- Ten lepers (Luke 17:11–19)
- Malchus's ear (Luke 22:50–51; John 18:10)
- Capernaum official's son in Cana (John 4:46–54)
- Man at Bethesda pool (John 5:1–9)
- Man born blind (John 9:1–7)

Freeing People Affected by Demons
- At Peter's house (Matthew 8:16)
- Two men from Gadarenes (Matthew 8:28–34)
- Mute man (Matthew 9:32–33)
- Blind and mute man (Matthew 12:22)
- Boy with seizures (Matthew 17:14–19)
- Man in synagogue (Mark 1:21–28)
- General casting out (Mark 1:39; 3:11)
- Syro-Phoenician woman's daughter (Mark 7:24–30)
- Some of Jesus' female followers (Luke 8:2)
- Seven demons from Mary Magdalene (Luke 8:2)

Exercising Authority over Nature
- Calming the storm (Matthew 8:23–27)
- Feeding 5,000 (Matthew 14:13–21)
- Walking on water (Matthew 14:23–33)
- Feeding 4,000 (Matthew 15:32–38)
- Four-drachma coin in fish's mouth (Matthew 17:24–27)
- Cursing fig tree (Matthew 21:18–19)
- Miraculous escape (Luke 4:28–30)
- Miraculous catch of fish (Luke 5:1–7; John 21:1–8)
- Water into wine (John 2:1–11)

Raising the Dead
- Raising the synagogue leader's daughter from the dead (Matthew 9:18–19, 23–25)
- Raising a widow's son from the dead (Luke 7:11–16)
- Raising Lazarus from the dead (John 11:38–44)

IDENTITY OF CHRIST

During his lifetime, who does Jesus claim to be? Does his life align with his words, proving him to be who he says he is? Obviously, the disciples think so, giving up their lives to follow the Son of God, the Savior of the world. Today, over two thousand years after Jesus' death, his followers still gather in communities throughout the world, worshiping him as the Son of the living God.

Jesus Is the Lamb of God

At the beginning of Jesus' public ministry on earth, he approaches his cousin, John the Baptist, at the Jordan River. John is "preparing the way" for the Messiah through preaching a message of repentance, calling people to repent from their sins and be baptized. When John sees Jesus approaching him, he cries out, "Look, the Lamb of God, who takes away the sin of the world!" (John 1:29).

Throughout Israel's history, God requires his people to make atonement for their sins. They do this by sacrificing burnt offerings of animals such as lambs, goats, and doves. Once a year, on the Day of Atonement, Israel's high priest enters into the Holy of Holies, where he offers the sacrifice of a perfect, unblemished lamb to God. When Jesus comes, he is the perfect sacrifice and the great High Priest who ushers in the way of salvation. Jesus lives a sinless life and offers "for all time one sacrifice for sins" (Hebrews 10:12; see also 10:5 – 13). That offering is his body, which he willingly yields to death on the cross. Jesus, the Lamb of God, dies on the cross in our place in order to pay for our sins. After his death and resurrection, he ascends to heaven, where he sits at the right hand of the Father (Hebrews 10:12).

Jesus Is "God with Us"

Jesus is God incarnate, God made flesh (John 1:1, 14). He is the One whom the prophet Isaiah foretold 700 years before his birth, saying that he would be called Immanuel, meaning "God with us" (Matthew 1:23; Isaiah 7:14). Although the Bible conveys that God living among us is an incomprehensible mystery (1 Timothy 3:16),

Identity of Jesus

Is God incarnate
Matt. 1:23; John 1:14;
1 Tim. 3:16

Has divine authority
Matt. 28:19;
John 10:30;
14:9 – 11

Has power over nature
Matt. 14:25;
Luke 8:23 – 25

Is omnipotent
Col 1:16

Is eternal
John 8:58;
10:28

Is omniscient
Matt. 16:21; 17:27;
John 1:47 – 49; 4:16 – 18

Forgives sins
Mark 2:3 – 5;
Luke 7:48 – 49

Is omnipresent
Matt. 18:20;
28:20

Is our rock
Rom. 9:33; 1 Cor. 10:1 – 4

Is our light
John
1:4 – 9;
8:12

Is our Savior
Luke 2:11;
Phil. 3:20;
2 Tim. 1:10

Gives life to the dead
Matt. 9:23 – 25;
John 11:17 – 44

it is a mystery and truth that is revealed in Jesus.

From the beginning, God desires to have a loving relationship with his people. He creates people in his image and fellowships with them in the garden of Eden (Genesis 1:26–3:10). The coming of God in the flesh in the form of Jesus (John 3:16–17) demonstrates God's great love for humanity. He has never forsaken his people (Hebrews 13:5), and he has not left us as orphans (John 14:18). The God of the universe has come to redeem us so that we might be with him, enjoying his presence as humanity once did in the garden of Eden.

Jesus Is the Only Way to Salvation

As God, Jesus is eternal. He has neither a beginning nor an end. Jesus states, "Before Abraham was born, I am" (John 8:58). In this statement, Jesus claims to be the same God who spoke with Moses and told him to tell the Israelites that "I Am" had sent him (Exodus 3:14). As the eternal Son of God, Jesus promises eternal life to those who follow him (John 10:27–28).

Throughout his ministry, Jesus makes several claims about being the only way for people to receive forgiveness of sins and eternal life. He says, "I am the way and the truth and the life. No one comes to the Father except through me" (John 14:6). He claims to be the Living Water; those who drink of him will never thirst again (John 4:13–14). He claims to be the only gate by which people can enter into salvation (John 10:9). He claims to be the resurrection and the life; those who believe in him will never die (John 11:25–26).

The Bible reveals that simple faith in Jesus, faith like that of a child (Matthew 18:3), is the way to salvation: "If you declare with your mouth, 'Jesus is Lord,' and believe in your heart that God raised him from the dead, you will be saved" (Romans 10:9).

Jesus Is the Messiah, the Son of the Living God

After ministering with the twelve disciples for almost three years, Jesus poses the question of his identity to his disciples: "Who do people say the Son of Man is?" The disciples reply, "Some say John the Baptist; others say Elijah; and still others, Jeremiah or one of the prophets." Jesus then asks, "But what about you? Who do you say I am?" When Simon Peter answers, "You are the Messiah, the Son of the living God," Jesus praises him, telling him that he is blessed with knowledge that can be revealed to him only from the Father in heaven (Matthew 16:13–17).

He has complete, divine authority over everything in heaven and on earth. Jesus demonstrates this authority on many occasions throughout Scripture. He performs miracles that no one other than God can do. He demonstrates power over the forces of nature by walking on the water (Matthew 14:25), calming storms with just a word (Luke 8:22–25), and ultimately by rising from the dead after three days as he said he would: "Destroy this temple, and I will raise it again in three days" (John 2:19).

Jesus' authority comes from the fact that he is both from the Father and one with the Father. "I and the Father are one," Jesus states (John 10:30). When his disciples ask Jesus to show them God, he explains that if they have seen him, they have seen the Father (John 14:9). Many of the people who doubt Jesus' identity ask him to tell them plainly if he is the Messiah. Jesus responds that his identity is clearly revealed through his life: "The works I do in my Father's name testify about me" (John 10:25).

As the Son of the Living God, Jesus has the authority on earth to forgive sins. Throughout his three years of ministry, Jesus supports this claim. For example, before healing a paralyzed man, Jesus tells him, "Son, your sins are forgiven" (Mark 2:5). The teachers of the law accuse Jesus in their hearts of blaspheming, arguing, "Who can forgive sins, but God alone?" They fail to recognize that Jesus is God incarnate. Jesus responds, "Which is easier: to say to this paralyzed man, 'Your sins are forgiven,' or to say, 'Get up, take your mat and walk'? But I want you to know that the Son of Man has authority on earth to forgive sins" (Mark 2:9 – 10). At this, the paralyzed man stands up and walks, astonishing the crowd.

As the Messiah, Jesus has incomparable power, "above all rule and authority, power and dominion" (Ephesians 1:21). Not only does Jesus have power over the wind and the waves, but as the author of life, Jesus has power over death. On three occasions, Jesus resurrects the dead. In every instance, many witnesses observe that the person is dead before Jesus tells them to rise (Matthew 9:23 – 25; Luke 7:11 – 15; John 11:17 – 344, esp. 42). Jesus calls for his friend Lazarus to rise from the dead after he has been in a tomb for four days (John 11:39).

Ultimately, Jesus proves his power over death when he rises from the dead on the third day after his crucifixion. He tells his disciples that this will happen on several occasions (Matthew 20:17 – 19; Mark 8:31 – 38; Matthew 16:21 – 28; Mark 10:32 – 34; John 10:11). Despite being told several times that Jesus must die and rise again, the disciples fail to grasp what Jesus teaches them about his death and resurrection until after he dies, rises again, and explains to them from the Scriptures that all of these things were necessary to fulfill his reason for coming — to redeem people to himself.

Jesus has the authority to command the obedience of his disciples. He tells his followers that in order to be his disciples, they must deny themselves, pick up their crosses, and follow him (Mark 8:34). When giving his disciples the Great Commission to take the gospel, or the good news, into the entire world, Jesus makes it clear that all authority, both in heaven and on earth, has been given to him (Matthew 28:18 – 20). He, in turn, sends his Holy Spirit to his followers in order to continue his works on earth (John 14:16, 26; 15:26; 16:7).

Through the power of the Holy Spirit, the good news that faith in Jesus can save us from our sins has been spreading throughout the world for more than two thousand years. It will continue to spread until "every tribe and language and people and nation" has heard (Revelation 5:9; 13:7). Then Jesus will return, making "everything new" (Revelation 21:5), restoring humanity, heaven, and earth to God's intended state of harmony and perfection.

REACTION TO JESUS

Everywhere Jesus goes, he elicits strong reactions from people. No one can remain neutral in his presence. Some people respond by immediately putting their faith and trust in him, doing as he tells them or following him wherever he goes. Others are deeply offended by his words, some even calling out, "Stone him!"

When Jesus calls his disciples, they immediately leave their families and their work to follow him. They don't hesitate. For example, when Andrew meets Jesus, he quickly concludes that he has found the Messiah. He looks for his brother, Simon (later Simon Peter), to bring him to Jesus (John 1:40–42). Simon Peter later responds to Jesus' question about who people think he is by declaring that Jesus is the Messiah (Luke 9:20). Jesus tells Peter that he is blessed because that knowledge can be

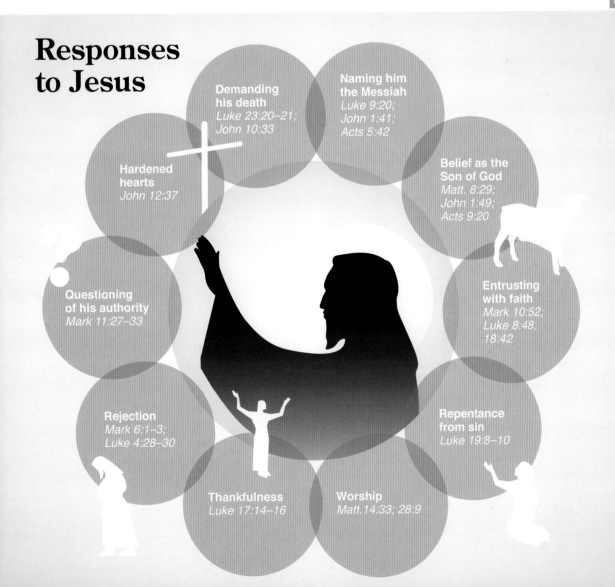

Responses to Jesus

Demanding his death
Luke 23:20–21;
John 10:33

Naming him the Messiah
Luke 9:20;
John 1:41;
Acts 5:42

Belief as the Son of God
Matt. 8:29;
John 1:49;
Acts 9:20

Hardened hearts
John 12:37

Entrusting with faith
Mark 10:52;
Luke 8:48;
18:42

Questioning of his authority
Mark 11:27–33

Repentance from sin
Luke 19:8–10

Rejection
Mark 6:1–3;
Luke 4:28–30

Thankfulness
Luke 17:14–16

Worship
Matt. 14:33; 28:9

EVENTS AND STORY LINE

revealed only from heaven. After Jesus' resurrection, the apostles are certain enough that Jesus is the Messiah that they are willing to continue proclaiming this truth even after being beaten for speaking in Jesus' name (Acts 5:42).

The apostle Paul, who originally persecuted Christians, preaches that Jesus is the Son of God after he has a dramatic experience in which Jesus speaks to him and blinds him on the road to Damascus (Acts 9:1–6, 20–22).

Some people respond to Jesus in faith and receive the healing or the miracle that they are seeking. This group of people includes at least two blind men who receive their sight (Luke 18:35–42; Mark 10:46–52) and a woman who is healed of an incurable bleeding condition when she touches Jesus' cloak (Luke 8:43–48).

Other people respond to Jesus in repentance, seeking forgiveness for the wrongs they have done. When meeting Jesus, a tax collector immediately repents for stealing money and offers to repay anyone he has cheated (Luke 19:8–10).

Others respond to Jesus with deep gratitude and sincere worship. One woman pours a bottle of perfume on Jesus' feet and weeps. Then, using her hair and her tears, she kisses his feet and wipes them clean (Luke 7:37–38). This intimate expression of worship is condemned by the Jewish leaders who witness it, but the woman is praised by Jesus, saying, "Your sins are forgiven.... Your faith has saved you; go in peace" (Luke 7:48, 50). When Jesus' disciples see him calm a storm by speaking to it, they, like the woman,

also respond by worshiping him (Matthew 14:33). When they see him after his resurrection, they fall at his feet, worshiping him (Matthew 28:9).

Other people respond to Jesus less favorably. For example, many of the elders, priests, and teachers of the law in Jerusalem respond to Jesus' cleansing of the temple by questioning his authority (Mark 11:27–33) or wanting him thrown out or even killed. Many people witness Jesus' miracles and still refuse to believe in him (John 12:37). Others believe in him but keep silent about their belief because they're afraid of being put out of the synagogue (John 12:42–43).

On several occasions, people react so strongly to Jesus that they call for his death. People in his hometown of Nazareth are quick to dismiss Jesus because he is the son of a local carpenter and they know his family (Mark 6:1–6). When Jesus points out that no prophet is accepted in his hometown, the people of Nazareth become so angry that they try to throw him off a cliff (Luke 4:14–30).

The people of Jerusalem attempt to stone Jesus for calling God his Father and claiming to be one with the Father. When Jesus challenges them to judge him by his works, they accuse him of blasphemy, saying that he is calling himself God (John 10:22–39).

The harshest reaction to, and the ultimate rejection of, Jesus comes when he is handed over to the Roman governor, Pilate. Crowds, many of whom have heard him teach and seen his miraculous works, demand that Pilate have Jesus crucified (Luke 23:20–21), which Pilate does.

TRANSFIGURATION

Approximately one week after Peter declares that Jesus is the Messiah, the Son of the living God (Matthew 16:16), Jesus brings him, James, and John up on a high mountain to pray (Luke 9:28). While they are there, Jesus' appearance changes. His face suddenly shines like the sun and his clothes become bright and unnaturally white, like lightning (Luke 9:29; Matthew 17:2).

Two men, whom the disciples recognize as Moses and the prophet Elijah, suddenly appear with Jesus. While the disciples watch in awe, Jesus begins speaking with Moses and Elijah about his impending death in Jerusalem (Luke 9:30–31). When Elijah and Moses begin to leave, Peter suggests building three shelters — one for Jesus, one for Moses, and one for Elijah — so they can stay on the mountain longer (Luke 9:32–34). When Peter suggests this, a bright cloud covers the three of them and a voice from heaven says: "This is my Son, whom I love. Listen to him!" (Mark 9:7). When Peter, James, and John look again, they see no one but Jesus (Mark 9:7–8).

This experience proves to the other two disciples what Peter has recently declared: that Jesus is the Son of God, the promised and long-awaited Messiah. Jesus is greater than the Law, represented by Moses, and the Prophets, represented by Elijah. In fact, Jesus says at one point in his ministry, "Do not think that I have come to abolish the Law or the Prophets; I have not come to abolish them but to fulfill them" (Matthew 5:17).

After Moses and Elijah have gone, Jesus instructs Peter, James, and John not to tell anyone what they have seen until after he has risen from the dead. The disciples discuss this among themselves, not understanding what Jesus means when he speaks about his coming resurrection (Mark 9:10).

Later, Peter recounts Jesus' transfiguration in his second letter (2 Peter). He emphasizes that the things he says about Jesus are from an eyewitness account. He saw Jesus glorified and heard the voice from heaven declaring that Jesus is God's Son (2 Peter 1:16–18).

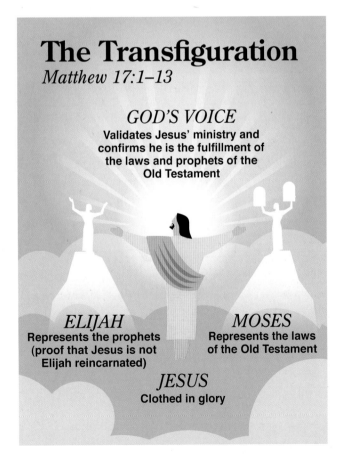

The Transfiguration
Matthew 17:1–13

GOD'S VOICE
Validates Jesus' ministry and confirms he is the fulfillment of the laws and prophets of the Old Testament

ELIJAH
Represents the prophets (proof that Jesus is not Elijah reincarnated)

MOSES
Represents the laws of the Old Testament

JESUS
Clothed in glory

TRIUMPHAL ENTRY

The Triumphal Entry into Jerusalem marks the height of Jesus' favor with the people of Jerusalem. Yet his reception by the crowds sets in motion the events that lead to his arrest, trial, and crucifixion.

As Jesus enters Jerusalem riding a young donkey, the crowds praise him, waving palm branches, laying their coats before him on the road, and singing, "Hosanna," meaning "we rejoice" or "we praise." The Pharisees demand that Jesus stop the people from celebrating him, but Jesus tells them that the rocks would cry out if the people remained silent.

As Jesus gets close to Jerusalem, he weeps, realizing the same people will soon reject him. He prophesies that Jerusalem will be destroyed by her enemies, a prophecy fulfilled in AD 70 when the Romans besiege Jerusalem (Luke 19:41–44).

Triumphal Entry
Mark 11:1–11

JERUSALEM:
Jesus fulfills Old Testament prophecy by entering Jerusalem as the King of Israel
Zech. 9:9

SONG OF THE PEOPLE:
As Jesus enters Jerusalem, the people sing, "Hosanna," a Hebrew expression meaning "save!"
see Psalm 118:25–26

COLT:
Jesus rode a young donkey that has never been ridden or used in labor, which symbolizes an offering and indicates that Jesus is arriving to the city as a peaceful king

PALM BRANCHES:
The people spread palm branches on the road to symbolize victory

CLOAKS PAVING THE ROAD:
The people lay their garments on the road before Jesus to symbolize their submission to him as King

JESUS' FINAL WEEK

The final week of Jesus' life is known as "the Passion," meaning agony or suffering. Scripture doesn't provide exact dates for many of these events (Matthew 21–27; Mark 11–15; Luke 19:28–23:56; and John 12–19).

At the beginning of the week, the crowds in Jerusalem celebrate Jesus' arrival, cheering and lining the streets with palm branches as he rides into the city on a young donkey (Matthew 21:1–11). The next day, Jesus angers the Jewish leaders by driving merchants out of the temple for turning his Father's house into a "den of robbers" (Matthew 21:12–46).

Jesus spends the following day teaching his disciples, warning them to remain faithful and prepare for his second coming (Matthew 22–25). By midweek, Jewish leaders bribe one of the disciples, Judas Iscariot, in exchange for information about where Jesus can be found. For a mere 30 pieces of silver, Judas betrays Jesus (Matthew 26:14–16). The next night, while Jesus is sharing a Passover meal (later known to Christians as the Last Supper) with the disciples, Judas leaves to betray Jesus. Jesus spends the first part of the evening in solitary prayer in the garden of Gethsemane before Judas arrives there with an armed crowd to capture Jesus (Matthew 26:17–75). They arrest Jesus, handing him over to the authorities to suffer and die.

On Thursday, the Roman prefect, Pontius Pilate, attempts to release Jesus, but the crowd is in an uproar. He orders Jesus' crucifixion as the Jewish people, spurred on by their leaders, repeatedly shout, "Crucify him!"

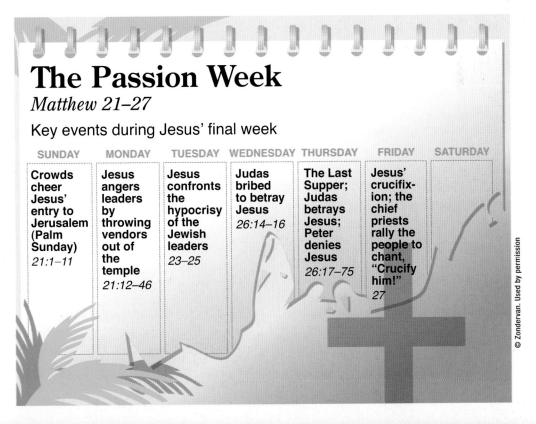

The Passion Week
Matthew 21–27

Key events during Jesus' final week

SUNDAY	MONDAY	TUESDAY	WEDNESDAY	THURSDAY	FRIDAY	SATURDAY
Crowds cheer Jesus' entry to Jerusalem (Palm Sunday) 21:1–11	Jesus angers leaders by throwing vendors out of the temple 21:12–46	Jesus confronts the hypocrisy of the Jewish leaders 23–25	Judas bribed to betray Jesus 26:14–16	The Last Supper; Judas betrays Jesus; Peter denies Jesus 26:17–75	Jesus' crucifixion; the chief priests rally the people to chant, "Crucify him!" 27	

© Zondervan. Used by permission

DEATH AND RESURRECTION

Shortly after Peter professes that Jesus is the Messiah of God (Luke 9:18–20), Jesus again tells his followers that he must suffer, be rejected by the church leaders, be killed, and then be raised to life on the third day. He then explains that anyone who wants to be his disciple must take up his or her cross and follow him (Luke 9:21–23).

Jesus' crucifixion begins with a brutal beating, wearing a crown of thorns, and carrying his own crossbeam through the city to the place of his execution. While Jesus is dying, the land becomes supernaturally dark. Around three in the afternoon, Jesus cries out in Hebrew, quoting from Psalm 22: "My God, my God, why have you forsaken me?" (Matthew 27:45–46). At this moment, Jesus is taking upon himself all of humanity's sin, as well as all of God's wrath, mysteriously experiencing complete separation from the Father.

In John's account of the crucifixion, he records Jesus' last words as "It is finished," after which Jesus "bowed his head and gave up his spirit" (John 19:28–30). These words signify the accomplishment of the Father's will in reconciling humanity to himself. The cross of Christ, the blood of the Lamb, now provides direct access to a holy and loving God.

When Jesus dies, the earth shakes, rocks split, tombs open, and the massive veil in the Holy of Holies in the Jerusalem temple is split from top to bottom (Matthew 27:51–52). Jesus is then placed inside of a cave-like tomb secured by a large boulder and guarded by two Roman soldiers (Mark 15:42–47; Matthew 27:62–66). On the third day after Jesus' death, an angel with an "appearance like lightning" and "clothes

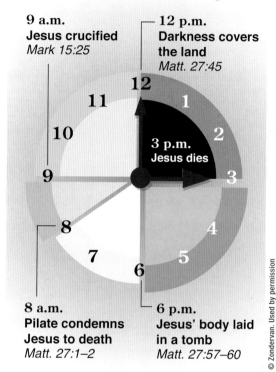

Good Friday

9 a.m.
Jesus crucified
Mark 15:25

12 p.m.
Darkness covers the land
Matt. 27:45

3 p.m.
Jesus dies

8 a.m.
Pilate condemns Jesus to death
Matt. 27:1–2

6 p.m.
Jesus' body laid in a tomb
Matt. 27:57–60

© Zondervan. Used by permission

as white as snow" appears at the tomb. The guards are so afraid, they become "like dead men." To the women at Jesus' tomb who had come to tend to his body, the angel says, "Do not be afraid . . . He is not here; he has risen, just as he said" (Matthew 28:5–6).

The angel then tells the women to go and tell the disciples the news: Jesus "has risen from the dead and is going ahead of you into Galilee. There you will see him" (Matthew 28:7). As the women report this news to the disciples, Jesus appears to them. They fall at his feet and worship him (Matthew 28:9). Jesus, the Author of life, now holds the keys of death and hades (Revelation 1:18).

Jesus' Crucifixion

Judas betrays JESUS
Luke 22:3–6

JESUS and the disciples share the Lord's Supper
Luke 22:19–20

JESUS prays in the Garden of Gethsemane
Mark 14:32–42

JESUS announces he will be crucified
Matt. 26:1–5

JESUS is arrested
Luke 22:47–54

A woman prepares JESUS' body for burial
Matt. 26:6–13

JESUS stands trial before the Jewish council
Mark 14:53–65

JESUS is rejected
Mark 15:6–15

JESUS is crucified
Mark 15:20–32

The temple curtain tears from top to bottom
Matt. 27:51a

The earth shakes, rocks split and tombs break open
Matt. 27:51b–52

ASCENSION AND FINAL WORDS

The earliest written account of the resurrection and ascension of Jesus appears not in the Gospels, but in 1 Corinthians 15, written by the apostle Paul. He indicates that Jesus appeared first to Cephas, or Peter, then to the apostles, and then to 500 other believers. It is very interesting that Paul begins with Peter, the rock, and then moves down to the other apostles and finally to unnamed believers. Paul counts himself as last in this process.

In the Gospels, Jesus first appears to the women who are visiting his tomb in order to anoint his dead body. When one of the women, Mary Magdalene, tells the disciples that Jesus is risen, they refuse to believe her (John 20:11–18; Mark 16:9–11). Jesus later rebukes the disciples for not trusting the testimony of those who told them about his resurrection (Mark 16:12–13).

Jesus also appears to two of the disciples as they walk to Emmaus. While the three walk, they recount the events leading to Jesus' death. Though Jesus explains the prophetic Scriptures to them, they don't recognize him until they eat together later (Luke 24:13–35).

Later, Jesus is sitting on the shore of the Sea of Galilee when the disciples return from fishing. Here Jesus forgives Peter for denying him and reaffirms Peter's calling to care for his followers.

Jesus' final words commission them to preach the good news throughout the world, making disciples of all nations and "baptizing them in the name of the Father and of the Son and of the Holy Spirit" (Matthew 28:19).

Crucifixion, Resurrection and Ascension

Commissions his disciples to spread the gospel
Matt. 28:18–20

Taken up into heaven
Mark 16:19

Appears to 500 believers
1 Cor. 15:1–11

Appears to disciples by the Sea of Galilee
John 21:1–13

Appears to Thomas
John 20:24–29

Appears to Mary Magdalene
John 20:14–18

Appears to disciples on the road to Emmaus
Luke 24:13–35

Resurrected
Matt. 28:1–8

Dies on the cross
Matt. 27:45–54

Speaks with Peter
John 21:15–24

Buried in a tomb
Luke 23:50–56

Crucified
Mark 15:20–32

PENTECOST

Before Jesus ascends to heaven, he tells his followers to stay in Jerusalem until they have been filled with the Holy Spirit (Acts 1:4–5) and "clothed with power from on high" (Luke 24:49).

On the day of Pentecost, the Jewish feast 50 days after Passover, the followers of Jesus receive the promised Spirit. They hear a mighty wind, see flames of fire above their heads, and speak in unknown languages. Many different nations such as the Persians, Egyptians, and Libyans are in the crowd.

For the first time, they hear the good news of Jesus' death on the cross and resurrection proclaimed in their native languages, a message they carry to their homelands.

The day of Pentecost marks the outpouring of the Holy Spirit onto Jesus' followers, empowering them to continue in the mission that he has given them. Jesus tells them that this "advocate," the Holy Spirit, will empower them to do not only what he has been doing while on earth, but "even greater things" because he goes to the Father (John 14:12).

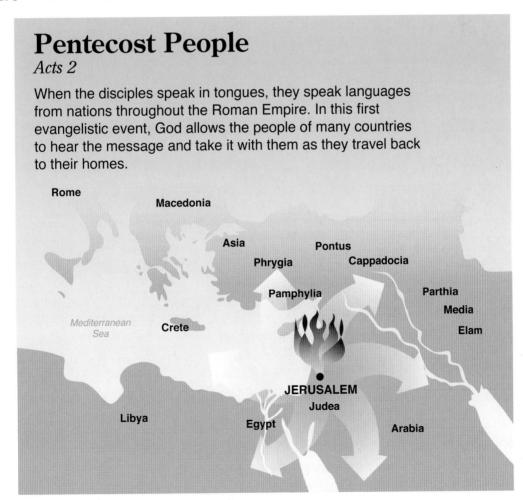

Pentecost People
Acts 2

When the disciples speak in tongues, they speak languages from nations throughout the Roman Empire. In this first evangelistic event, God allows the people of many countries to hear the message and take it with them as they travel back to their homes.

ACTS AND THE APOSTLES

The book of Acts records many teachings by the followers of Jesus that cover a variety of topics for Jewish, Christian, and pagan audiences.

The first sermon in Acts is Peter's explanation of the baptism of the Holy Spirit. Peter explains that this experience is the fulfillment of words spoken by the prophet Joel (Acts 2:14–21). He then proceeds to preach the message of Jesus, recounting his death and resurrection and encouraging hearers to repent and be baptized (Acts 2:14–40).

Peter calls Jewish people to repent and believe in Jesus the Messiah (Acts 3:12–26), teaches about healing with Jesus' authority (Acts 4:5–12), and preaches the message of salvation to Gentiles (Acts 10:28–47). Peter later preaches to the believers in Jerusalem, defending the inclusion of the Gentiles (Acts 11:4–18) and Paul's conviction that all are saved by grace and not by works of the law (Acts 15:7–11).

Stephen preaches the longest sermon recorded in Acts. Before the synagogue rulers in Jerusalem, Stephen recounts the salvation history of the Jews as recorded in Scripture, arguing that Jesus is the Messiah (Acts 7). This sermon outrages the rulers and they stone Stephen, making him the first Christian martyr.

In a brief sermon while in Jerusalem, James teaches that Gentile converts do not need to be circumcised, an Old Testament requirement for God's people, in order to be saved (Acts 15:13–21).

Acts records six of Paul's sermons, including three apologies for the Christian faith. In Ephesus, Paul encourages believers to remain faithful despite persecution (Acts 20:17–35). While in Jerusalem, he speaks of his dramatic ministry (Acts 21:1–21). Paul defends his faith before local rulers such as King Agrippa.

The Preachers
Acts 2–28

Bible characters who spend the most time preaching in Acts (based on number of verses):

9 James

52 Stephen

75 Peter

117 Paul

PETER'S IMPACT

Peter, or Cephas, which means "rock," is the first disciple to recognize Jesus as the long-awaited Savior or Messiah, "the Son of the Living God" (Matthew 16:16). He is famous for being the only disciple to walk on water and for his three denials of Jesus (Mark 14:66–72).

Jesus speaks to Peter these significant words of commission: "And I tell you that you are Peter, and on this rock I will build my church, and the gates of Hades will not overcome it" (Matthew 16:18).

After Jesus' ascension into heaven, Peter goes on to help establish the church in the Roman Empire, through preaching, composing two books of the Bible (1 and 2 Peter), and miraculous healings (Acts 3:1–16).

Peter's Words
Significant words Peter uses most often in his sermons and letters*

8 POWER
12 LIVE
10 HEAVEN
9 GRACE
12 GLORY
28 JESUS
14 SPIRIT
32 CHRIST
10 FAITH
9 CALLED
9 PROPHETS
74 GOD
11 LOVE
12 DAY
30 LORD
14 GOOD
31 ALL
10 TIME
8 SUFFER
18 HOLY
12 EVIL
17 NOW
9 LIVING
9 DEAD

*Does not include pronouns, prepositions, articles or other words like is, and, but, etc.

PERSECUTION AND MARTYRDOM

As the church grows in its impact, opposition against the church also increases in intensity.

One of the earliest accounts of persecution is the arrest of Peter and John by the Sanhedrin, the Jewish ruling council. They imprison the apostles and have them flogged (Acts 5:17–42).

Persecution increases further when the Sanhedrin arrests Stephen, a deacon of the church, accusing him of blasphemy. Stephen's defense of Jesus as the Messiah outrages his accusers and they stone him, making him the first Christian martyr (Acts 6:8–7:60).

Jewish leaders attempt to suppress the expansion of the early church by continuing to imprison believers. The disciples scatter from Jerusalem, carrying the gospel message throughout the world (Acts 8:1–3). Originally, Saul is among those seeking to arrest and kill believers. However, after an encounter with Jesus, Saul, later known as Paul, helps carry the good news to non-Jews, or Gentiles (Acts 8:1; 9:1–19; 1 Corinthians 15:9).

King Herod has the apostle James put to death. When the Jews express approval, Herod arrests Peter as well. Peter is saved from trial when an angel of the Lord miraculously frees him from prison (Acts 12:1–19).

On Paul's first missionary journey, Jews in Lystra drag him from the city and stone him, leaving him for dead (Acts 14:19–20).

Paul and Silas are later beaten and arrested in Philippi (Acts 16:20–24). Paul is ultimately imprisoned and brought to Rome before being beheaded.

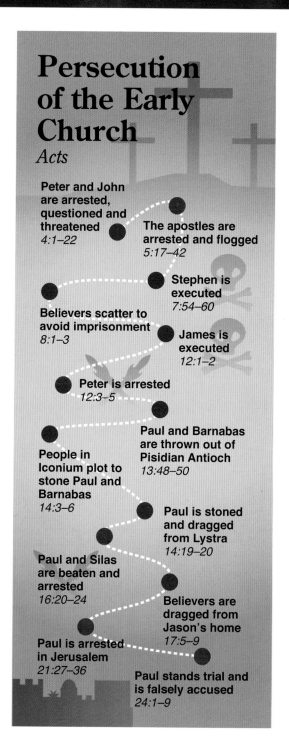

Persecution of the Early Church
Acts

Peter and John are arrested, questioned and threatened
4:1–22

The apostles are arrested and flogged
5:17–42

Stephen is executed
7:54–60

Believers scatter to avoid imprisonment
8:1–3

James is executed
12:1–2

Peter is arrested
12:3–5

Paul and Barnabas are thrown out of Pisidian Antioch
13:48–50

People in Iconium plot to stone Paul and Barnabas
14:3–6

Paul is stoned and dragged from Lystra
14:19–20

Paul and Silas are beaten and arrested
16:20–24

Believers are dragged from Jason's home
17:5–9

Paul is arrested in Jerusalem
21:27–36

Paul stands trial and is falsely accused
24:1–9

THE ROAD TO DAMASCUS

The biblical book of Acts, along with the letters to the early churches, known as epistles, tell the story of the life of Saul, a zealous Pharisee of Tarsus (Acts 21:39; 23:6–9; 26:5). In Scripture, we learn that Saul first studied under a rabbi named Gamaliel (Acts 22:3) before becoming a Pharisee (Acts 23:6). Saul is known for his zealous reverence for the law of God (Galatians 1:14). He first enters the biblical story during the stoning of Stephen, when the accusers lay their coats at Paul's feet. The writer of Acts makes a point to emphasize that Saul approves of the stoning (Acts 7:54–8:1).

After Stephen is killed, Saul goes from house to house searching for believers to imprison in order to destroy the church (Acts 8:3). He then receives permission from the Jewish authorities to travel to Damascus hunting believers to bring back to Jerusalem as prisoners (Acts 9:1–2).

While Saul is en route to Damascus, a light from heaven shines on him, knocking him to the ground. He hears a voice ask, "Saul, Saul, why do you persecute me?" (Acts 9:4). When Saul inquires who is speaking, Jesus reveals himself to Saul. Jesus then tells him to go into Damascus and wait for further instruction (Acts 9:5–6).

Although the men accompanying Saul hear the sound, they are unable to see Jesus. When Saul rises from the ground, he is blind. His companions lead him to Damascus, where he fasts for three days (Acts 9:7–9). Saul spends time waiting and praying in the place where Jesus commanded him to go. While praying, he sees a vision of a man named Ananias laying hands on him and restoring his eyesight (Acts 9:10–12).

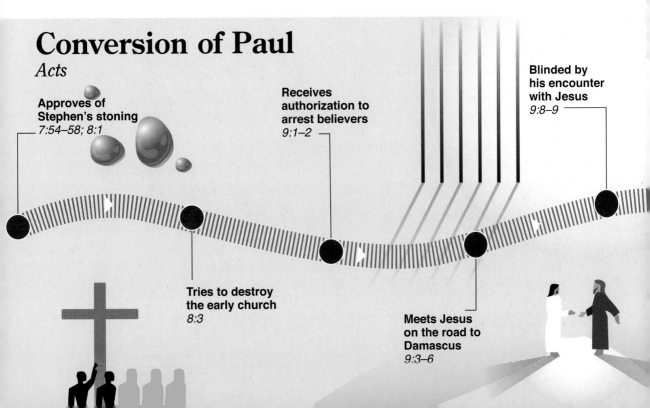

Conversion of Paul
Acts

**Approves of
Stephen's stoning**
7:54–58; 8:1

**Tries to destroy
the early church**
8:3

**Receives
authorization to
arrest believers**
9:1–2

**Meets Jesus
on the road to
Damascus**
9:3–6

**Blinded by
his encounter
with Jesus**
9:8–9

Soon, Ananias arrives and tells Saul that Jesus sent him to restore Saul's sight so that he may be filled with the Holy Spirit. During Ananias's prayer, "scales" fall from Saul's eyes; his sight is restored and he receives the Holy Spirit (Acts 9:17–19). Immediately, Saul begins preaching the message of Jesus throughout the synagogues of Damascus (Acts 9:20).

After his conversion, Saul exchanges the Hebrew version of his name for the Roman equivalent, Paul. As an apostle, Paul takes the gospel throughout the world, preaching to Gentiles, or non-Jews. Along with companions Barnabas, Mark, Silas, and Timothy, Paul establishes churches throughout Asia Minor, later writing several letters to the early churches, known as the epistles of Paul. (See chart below for a full list of Paul's writings.)

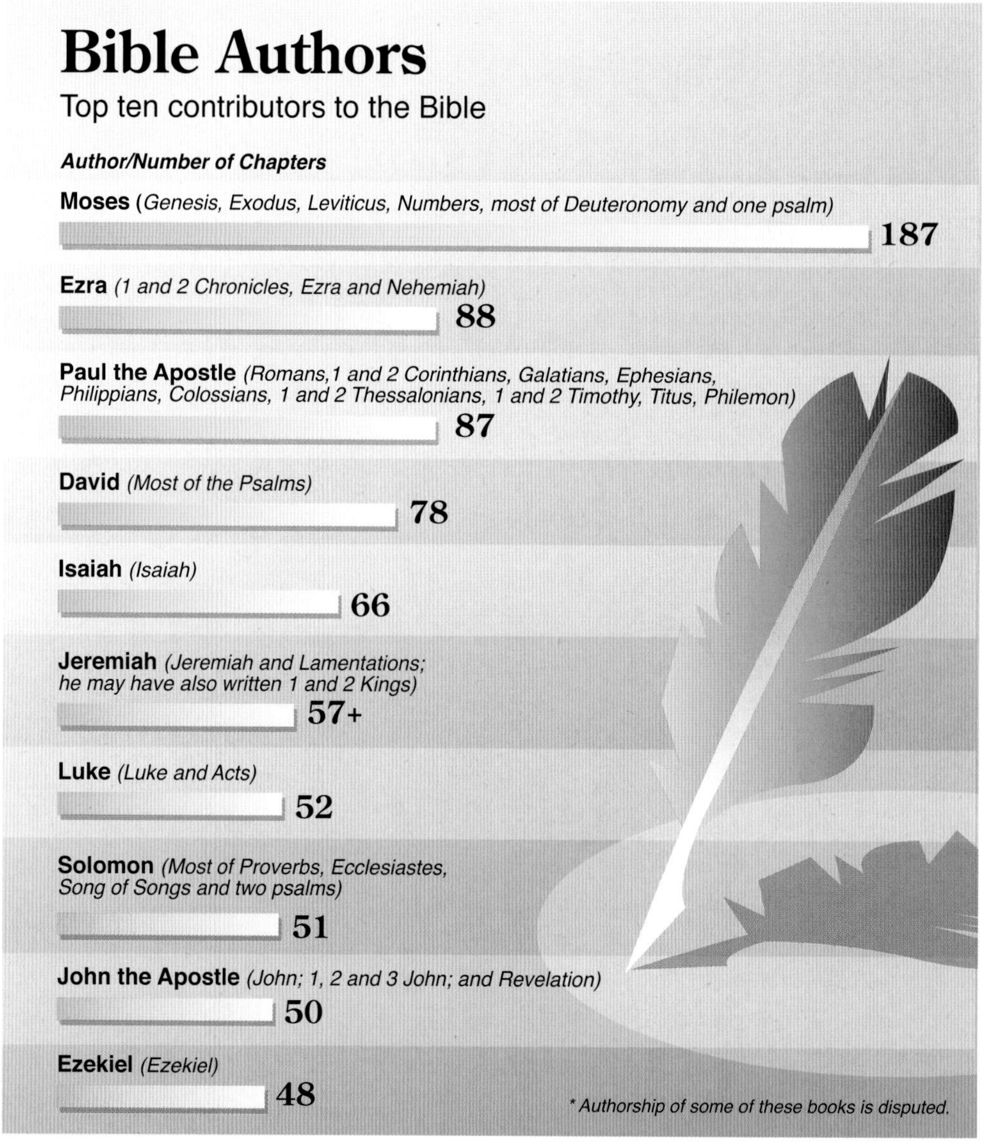

Bible Authors
Top ten contributors to the Bible

Author/Number of Chapters

Moses (*Genesis, Exodus, Leviticus, Numbers, most of Deuteronomy and one psalm*)
187

Ezra (*1 and 2 Chronicles, Ezra and Nehemiah*)
88

Paul the Apostle (*Romans, 1 and 2 Corinthians, Galatians, Ephesians, Philippians, Colossians, 1 and 2 Thessalonians, 1 and 2 Timothy, Titus, Philemon*)
87

David (*Most of the Psalms*)
78

Isaiah (*Isaiah*)
66

Jeremiah (*Jeremiah and Lamentations; he may have also written 1 and 2 Kings*)
57+

Luke (*Luke and Acts*)
52

Solomon (*Most of Proverbs, Ecclesiastes, Song of Songs and two psalms*)
51

John the Apostle (*John; 1, 2 and 3 John; and Revelation*)
50

Ezekiel (*Ezekiel*)
48

Authorship of some of these books is disputed.

PAUL'S MISSIONARY JOURNEYS

God says of Paul, "This man is my chosen instrument to proclaim my name to the Gentiles ... [and] the people of Israel" (Acts 9:15). Paul's life displays the power of God to transform a person from a persecutor of the church to one of its most effective missionaries. Paul's ministry spans many years, geographically covering almost the entire Roman Empire as Paul travels, teaches, and writes at least 13 books of the New Testament.

The First Journey

Paul's first missionary journey begins in Antioch approximately 13 years after his conversion around AD 47. The Holy Spirit speaks to the disciples during a time of worship and fasting, saying, "Set apart for me Barnabas and Saul for the work to which I have called them" (Acts 13:2). The disciples of Jesus fast, pray, and lay hands on Barnabas and Paul before sending them out to proclaim the gospel (Acts 13:3). The pair take Barnabas's cousin Mark, sometimes called John Mark or John, with them and travel to Seleucia and then to the island of Cyprus, where they visit the cities of Salamis and Paphos (Acts 13:4–6).

Paul, Barnabas, and Mark teach the gospel in the synagogues in Salamis (Acts 13:5). When they reach Paphos, the governor, Sergius Paulus, sends for Paul and Barnabas because he is curious about the word of God. While there, a Jewish sorcerer, who is an attendant of the governor, opposes them. Paul rebukes the sorcerer, who immediately loses his sight. Sergius Paulus becomes a believer as a result of seeing this miracle (Acts 13:6–12).

When the missionaries leave Paphos, they sail to Perga, on the southern coast of Galatia. While they are in Perga, John Mark parts company with Paul and Barnabas and returns to Jerusalem (Acts 13:13). Next, they go to Pisidian Antioch, where Paul preaches in the synagogues. Both Gentiles and Jews hear his message. He is so well received that most of the city comes to hear Paul and Barnabas preach. Jealous over their popularity, Jews in the city begin to

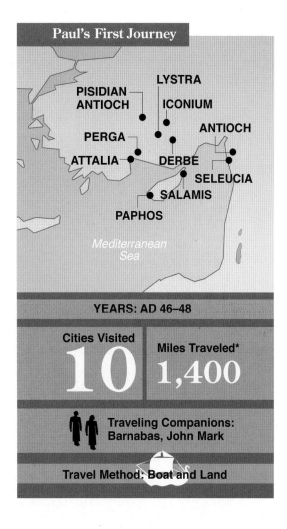

Paul's First Journey

LYSTRA
PISIDIAN ANTIOCH
ICONIUM
ANTIOCH
PERGA
ATTALIA
DERBE
SELEUCIA
SALAMIS
PAPHOS

Mediterranean Sea

YEARS: AD 46–48

Cities Visited
10

Miles Traveled*
1,400

Traveling Companions: Barnabas, John Mark

Travel Method: Boat and Land

oppose Paul (Acts 13:45). When they reject Paul and Barnabas's message, the missionaries declare that they will begin to preach the gospel to Gentiles instead. In this moment, Paul quotes Isaiah 49:6: "I have made you a light for the Gentiles, that you may bring salvation to the ends of the earth" (Acts 13:46–48).

Paul and Barnabas then journey to Iconium, Lystra, and Derbe, where they proclaim Jesus as Savior. After Paul heals a man lame since birth, the residents of Lystra conclude that he and Barnabas are gods and try to sacrifice to them. The people ultimately stone them and leave them for dead (Acts 14:8–20).

On their trip home, Barnabas and Paul return to cities they have already visited in order to strengthen the new followers of Jesus and to appoint elders over newly established churches. Then, they return to Syrian Antioch to report the results of their journey to the church that first sent them out (Acts 14:24–28).

The Second Journey

At one point during their missionary journeys, Paul and Barnabas have a disagreement over taking Mark with them. Barnabas ends up taking Mark to visit some churches while Paul takes another route with a new companion, Silas. During his second missionary journey, Paul is also accompanied by Timothy, Priscilla, and Aquila, and by Luke, who records many details of the ministry of Paul in Acts.

Paul visits the churches he and Barnabas established in Pisidian Antioch, Derbe, and Lystra. From there, they travel to Troas, on

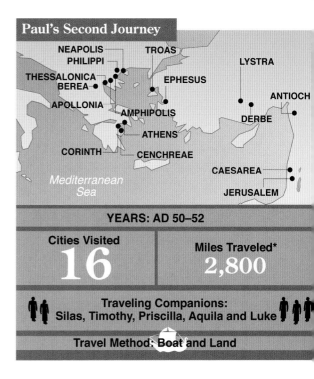

Paul's Second Journey

NEAPOLIS • TROAS • LYSTRA
PHILIPPI •
THESSALONICA • EPHESUS • ANTIOCH
BEREA •
APOLLONIA • AMPHIPOLIS • DERBE
ATHENS
CORINTH • CENCHREAE
Mediterranean Sea • CAESAREA
JERUSALEM

YEARS: AD 50–52

Cities Visited	Miles Traveled*
16	**2,800**

Traveling Companions:
Silas, Timothy, Priscilla, Aquila and Luke

Travel Method: Boat and Land

the west coast of Asia Minor. There, Paul sees a vision of a man from Macedonia pleading for his help. Paul responds by visiting a total of 16 cities in Galatia and Greece, preaching and establishing churches. While in the Greek city of Philippi, Paul and Silas are imprisoned but miraculously freed, leading to the conversion of their jailer and his family (Acts 16:16–34).

The Third Journey

Paul takes Timothy and Luke with him on his third missionary journey, visiting the churches in Galatia, Phrygia, and Ephesus. He ends up staying in Ephesus for approximately three years, during which time it is speculated that Paul writes several of his letters that become books of the Bible.

While Paul is in Ephesus, his ministry

causes business to sharply decline for the tradesmen there. The businesses have been profiting from the production of idols of the goddess Artemis, also called Diana. At one point, a silversmith named Demetrius leads the craftsmen in a riot, seizing some of Paul's associates (Acts 19:23–41). This ultimately leads to Paul's departure. As Paul goes, he announces his intention to travel to Jerusalem, where the Lord has revealed to him that he will face hardship and imprisonment (Acts 20:13–37).

To Jerusalem, the "Holy City"

Paul and his traveling companions go through Macedonia and Troas before going on to Jerusalem. While they are in Troas, a young man falls asleep during a sermon of Paul's and falls out of a window. Paul then raises the young man from the dead.

When Paul arrives in Jerusalem, he spends time with James and other church leaders. Paul had previously taken a strong stance against requiring Gentile converts to obey Jewish ceremonial laws, but there in the Holy City he submits to the elders' request that he purify himself according to

Jewish Old Testament law in order to avoid offending Jewish converts to Christ.

When some of the Jews see Paul in the temple, they falsely assume that he has brought Gentiles into the temple, so they try to kill him. Roman soldiers rescue Paul and allow him to preach to the crowd. When this causes further rioting, Paul is arrested. The soldiers' commander orders them to flog Paul, but relents when Paul informs them that he is a Roman citizen, since Roman citizens generally were not treated as harshly as noncitizens (Acts 21–22).

To Rome, the Center of Power

Paul's arrest leads to his transfer to Caesarea under armed guard. He is then imprisoned and tried twice (Acts 24–25). During the second trial, the governor asks Paul if he is willing to stand trial in Jerusalem. Paul, knowing that some Jews there intend to kill him, appeals to Caesar—his right as a Roman citizen—and is instead eventually sent to Rome. Under house arrest there, Paul ministers, writes several letters, and, according to church tradition, is eventually martyred.

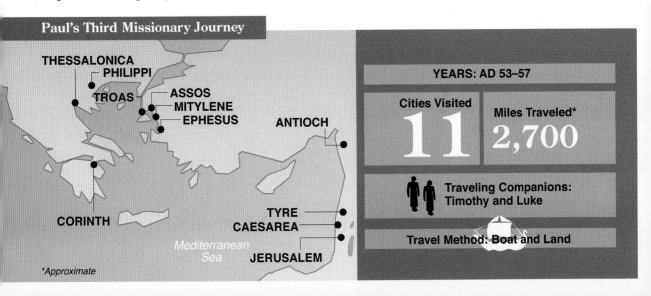

Paul's Third Missionary Journey

THESSALONICA
PHILIPPI
TROAS
ASSOS
MITYLENE
EPHESUS
ANTIOCH
CORINTH
TYRE
CAESAREA
Mediterranean Sea
JERUSALEM

*Approximate

YEARS: AD 53–57

Cities Visited
11

Miles Traveled*
2,700

Traveling Companions: Timothy and Luke

Travel Method: Boat and Land

NEW JERUSALEM

The Bible book of Revelation consists of a series of visions and prophecies seen by the apostle John while he is exiled on Patmos, a small Greek island in the Aegean Sea. Many of these visions focus on the end times and the ultimate fate of humankind.

Previously, while Jesus walked with his disciples on earth, he described his Father's house, which contains "many rooms." Jesus told them that he was going to prepare a place for them to live there (John 14:1–3). In Revelation, God provides John with an intimate glimpse into the place that is being prepared for him and for all who put their faith and trust in Jesus as Lord and Savior.

An angel, "one of the seven angels who had the seven bowls full of the seven last plagues" (Revelation 21:9), takes John on a guided tour through the city while John records its major features. From the outside, John notices that the gates never shut because night never comes, and that the city contains 12 gates with 12 angels at the gates, and that the gates bear the names of the 12 tribes of Israel. The wall of the city also has 12 foundations bearing the names of Jesus' 12 apostles (Revelation 21: 9–14).

The angel guiding John possesses a golden measuring stick with which he measures the city as 12,000 stadia, or roughly 1,400 miles, wide, long, and high, with walls approximately 200 feet thick. John marvels. The city is a cube (Revelation 21:16–17). Precious metals and gems enshrine New Jerusalem, a city with streets of gold so pure, it is transparent (Revelation 21:18, 21), with walls of unblemished jasper (Revelation 21:18), with foundations each decorated with a unique, precious gem (Revelation 21:19–20), and with individual gates each carved out of a single, enormous pearl (Revelation 21:21).

Every part of the New Jerusalem radiates with God's glory—the sun, moon, and any other artificial light all become unnecessary as God's light permeates everything, eradicating all shadows (Revelation 21:23; 22:5).

Within the city, God the Almighty with Jesus Christ, the Lamb of God, is the only temple to be found (Revelation 21:22). John goes on to write that only those whose names are written in the Lamb's book of life can enter the New Jerusalem (Revelation 21:27).

The throne of God and of the Lamb resides within the city, with the river of the water of life flowing from it and onto the city's streets of gold. The tree of life stands on both sides of the river, producing a new crop every month of the year.

When the end times come as described in Revelation, God will establish a perfect order to the universe. God alone rules the New Jerusalem, and all true believers in him will serve him. John's visions reveal that God's people will finally be able to see God face-to-face. His name will be written on the foreheads of all his children in the city. New Jerusalem, with its unparalleled riches, opportunities to worship, and fullness of God's presence, provides a new and final home beyond our wildest imagination. There God's people will enjoy a life described as one in which "'he will wipe every tear from their eyes. There will be no more death' or mourning or crying or pain, for the old order of things has passed away" (Revelation 22:4).

The New Jerusalem
Revelation 21:10—22:2

12 gates with names of 12 tribes of Israel

12 foundations with names of 12 apostles

City is shaped like a cube

12 angels at the gates

Walls of jasper; city of gold

Foundations of walls decorated with 12 kinds of jewels

Pearl gates; gold street

Temple is God and the Lamb

No moon or sun because the glory of God and the Lamb provide light

Only those whose names are written in the Lamb's book of life can enter

River of life flows from the throne of God and the Lamb

Tree of life stands on each side of the river

INDEX